THE TRUTH
OF SPIRITS

Hay House Titles of Related Interest

YOU CAN HEAL YOUR LIFE, the movie,
starring Louise Hay & Friends
(available as an online streaming video)
www.hayhouse.com/louise-movie

THE SHIFT, the movie,
starring Dr. Wayne W. Dyer
(available as an online streaming video)
www.hayhouse.com/the-shift-movie

~ ❧

*Don't Let Anything Dull Your Sparkle: How to Break Free of
Negativity and Drama,* by Doreen Virtue

*How to Love Yourself (and Sometimes Other People): Spiritual Advice for
Modern Relationships,* by Meggan Watterson and Lodro Rinzler

Life Loves You: 7 Spiritual Practices to Heal Your Life,
by Louise Hay and Robert Holden, Ph.D.

Remembering the Future: The Path to Recovering Intuition,
by Colette Baron-Reid

*Shadows Before Dawn: Finding the Light of Self-Love
Through Your Darkest Times,* by Teal Swan

All of the above are available at your local bookstore,
or may be ordered by visiting:

Hay House USA: www.hayhouse.com®
Hay House Australia: www.hayhouse.com.au
Hay House UK: www.hayhouse.co.uk
Hay House India: www.hayhouse.co.in

THE TRUTH OF SPIRITS

A Medium's Journey from Panic to Peace

CARMEL JOY BAIRD
with Tiffany Grabski

HAY HOUSE, INC.
Carlsbad, California • New York City
London • Sydney • New Delhi

Published in the United States by: Hay House, Inc.: www.hayhouse.com®
Published in Australia by: Hay House Australia Pty. Ltd.: www.hayhouse.com.au
Published in the United Kingdom by: Hay House UK, Ltd.: www.hayhouse.co.uk
Published in India by: Hay House Publishers India: www.hayhouse.co.in

Project editor: Nicolette Salamanca Young
Cover design: Michelle Polizzi • *Interior design:* Nick C. Welch

The Library of Congress has cataloged the earlier edition as follows:

Names: Baird, Carmel Joy, date.
Title: The truth of spirits : a medium's journey from panic to peace / Carmel
   Joy Baird, with Tiffany Grabski.
Description: 1st edition. | Carlsbad : Hay House, Inc., 2016.
Identifiers: LCCN 2015037304 | ISBN 9781401947620 (hardcover : alk. paper)
Subjects: LCSH: Baird, Carmel Joy, date. | Women mediums--Biography. |
   Spirits.
Classification: LCC BF1283.B33 A3 2016 | DDC 133.9/1092--dc23 LC record available
at http://lccn.loc.gov/2015037304

Tradepaper ISBN: 978-1-4019-4790-3

1st edition, March 2016
2nd edition, March 2017

Printed in the United States of America

I dedicate this book to my children, who have lovingly stuck with me throughout my journey and courageously picked me in this lifetime to be their mom; to my husband, Dave, who understands me and loves me for who I am, dead people and all; and to my mom, who never gave up on trying to understand me and gave me so much love and support on my healing journey. I love you and thank you all.

CONTENTS

INTRODUCTION

The Truth Within

This is my life story. In essence, it may not be very different from your own. Perhaps your path hasn't always been smooth; it certainly wasn't for me. This is a story about overcoming challenges, about stumbling but getting back up, and about finding the truth. It's a story about love, but also fear. It's about the nature of universal wisdom and how anyone can uncover their personal truth—their own authentic self.

Many people today (including, perhaps, you) are hiding the truth of who they really are in order to please those around them . . . it is such a common human experience that we share. I spent a long time hiding something *big*. Out of shame, I kept it from those around me as well as from myself—and this burden caused me great pain. What I was hiding wasn't something straightforward or commonplace. You might even have some difficulty relating to what I'm about to say, but I assure you that this is all true.

For most of my life, I hid my ability to *speak with the dead*. I didn't understand what the voices in my head were or why I was struck by unexplained, intense emotions around strangers. This confusion plagued me for years, and my denial of the truth caused me excruciating pain, panic, fear, and anxiety. When I finally let go of the shame and accepted my unusual gift, I found happiness, love . . . and even my own TV show!

The most important lesson that my gift has taught me, however, has been that the truth was within me all along. And this is something I hope each of you come to realize. *We are all the same.* Your inner truth may be different from my inner truth, but when you find and begin to live from your authentic self, the quality of your life will improve dramatically every day.

Living a Life in the Middle

My day job is to communicate with those who have passed away so that I can deliver their messages to the people they've left behind. I will refer to those who have passed on as Spirits. They are on the Other Side (as opposed to being on this side, with you and me here, on Earth).

It's like being a middleman, which is why I'm also called a medium! Some may think what I do isn't a "job," but believe it or not, it takes a lot of energy—mentally, physically, and emotionally—to connect with each and every Spirit that I come into contact with. In fact, every time I prepare to give someone a personal reading, I get a hint of the same anxiety that had taken over my life for years before I finally learned to control it.

What I have learned is that your loved ones on the Other Side go to great lengths to share messages with those of you still on this Earth, and each message has a purpose. The way they communicate to me varies. Sometimes I see pictures or visions, or I might hear sounds or smell distinct fragrances. Other times they'll interrupt my own thoughts with theirs, so I can hear their voices in my head. Imagine having *that* in your brain for years, and not knowing what it was! I truly thought I was crazy for most of my adult life. But now that I know what's going on, I have learned to interpret these symbols, feelings, smells, thoughts, visions, and whatever else comes through. Let's just say I've gotten really good at charades.

The Spirits themselves never lie or pass on inaccurate information—but sometimes my *interpretation* of the message can be wrong. (No pressure, right?!) Since I've never met these Spirits, I can't be 100 percent sure I'm catching every nuance. When they use a nickname, share an in-joke, or relay some unique aspect of their personality, I just pass along whatever I get, even if it doesn't seem to make sense to me. Even with the quirkiest message, I'll know I've got something when I see that incredulous look on my client's face. It's a sign that they understand the meaning and know that I am in touch with their loved one. So together we almost always figure it out, the message gets passed along through me—the medium—and the purpose of it all is always the same. It's to help us find the truth; the truth that was within us the whole time.

However, it took me nearly 30 years to finally realize my own truth—what was lurking behind my fears, panic, and anxiety. My journey led me to the realization that I am *not* crazy, and I never was. Perhaps the most dramatic thing I realized is that I'm really not much different from any of you. I believe that we *all* have the power to communicate with our loved ones who have passed on. In fact, I now teach others how to tap into this innate ability to communicate with the Other Side. What truly encouraged me to further develop this gift and turn it into my career came directly from my own life story: from the abuse, the fear, and the shame. Without it all, I wouldn't have been forced to find my own truth. That is why I want to share the story of my past. Without my past, as difficult as it was, I would not have my *present*.

The Four Truths

In discovering my own truth, I have also uncovered other universal truths that have completely transformed my life. So while the main narrative of this book covers my life story, I also share with you the lessons I learned along the way that you can use to transform your *own* life.

I have managed to unlock four truths that I now live by. They are the keys to life, keys that open us up to the reality of why we are here: love, peace, forgiveness, and balance. The whole reason for our existence is to learn and evolve as spiritual beings, and I believe these four truths to be the basis of it all. Without all four, we would still be able to live our divine purpose. But with them, we have the power to achieve our greatest dreams and to master what I call "the game of life."

So these are pretty heavy topics, and you might think to yourself: *My life is so mixed up right now. How am I going to suddenly discover the magic formula to love, peace, forgiveness, and balance?* That's a normal response. I'm not saying it happens suddenly or perfectly; goodness knows that life has not gone flawlessly for me! In fact, I am the first to admit I'm not perfect; no one is perfect, nor will we ever be. Each one of us will continuously work on bringing these four truths into our lives. Yet to know about and acknowledge these truths is the first step toward understanding the wisdom behind them and becoming a master of your own life.

Mastering the Truth of Love

Here is a glimpse of the immense value you will get when you master the truth of love. Once you accept love into all parts of your life, you will be able to love everyone and everything regardless of who or what they are, regardless of what they have done to you or what you have done to them. I really do mean absolutely anyone—even the "bad guys"! Imagine the freedom in this. Feel what that would be like, and you can begin to understand.

I have asked thousands of people if they believe that we are here on Earth to learn life lessons, and the response is almost always a resounding, "Yes!" That's when I ask "So if we were all *good,* then what would we learn from? Someone *has* to be the bad guy." Or at least, we like to call them that. But just to be clear, when I say "bad" I am viewing it as an *action*, not a *trait*.

People may harm us, but that does not make them *bad*, it makes them our teachers. How tragic it would be for the both of us if we don't accept these teachings—especially because, as Spirits on the Other Side, *we* picked the lessons we wanted to experience in this lifetime. Oh, I know what you're thinking. No one wants to hear that they *chose* the things that have happened to them. But it's true, my friend. You did it before you ever came into this world; when you can understand that, you will understand the truth behind love, and this truth will change your life forever. It certainly changed mine!

My story has no bad guys, although it may seem to you like it's riddled with them as you begin to read. I once thought my life was nothing but "bad guys," and I even counted myself among them from time to time. What I have come to learn is that each person, each difficulty, each lesson we encounter is a chance for us to find and more fully understand another aspect of our truths and to learn a new life lesson.

Some of the people in my life you meet in these pages may seem to be monsters, but the stronger their actions toward me, the more I have to thank them for. Without them, I wouldn't be who I am today—a person who helps people heal and reach their own truths as well.

In Search of Inner and Outer Peace

Now I dedicate my life to helping thousands of people connect with those on the Other Side and find peace, which is the second of the four truths. Both clients and Spirits come to me when they can't find peace. They are searching for a sign from someone they miss, or they desperately need to say something that was left unsaid at the time of death.

But before I was able to help others, I first had to master this truth myself. For me, this meant breaking out of a terrifying cage of fear and finding stillness within the present moment. Peace is a whisper, a floating feather. It's consciously noticing where you are and what is around you, and coming to terms with the way life is *in this very moment.*

Some of my life's greatest lessons were how I managed to overcome panic and find a peaceful place. It was the most amazing feeling, and I am so proud to now guide other people to find it within themselves. You'll find inspiration and techniques within my story that will help you as well. Another piece of good news is that once you find your way to inner peace, your outer world calms down, and it is a most miraculous and life-affirming feeling. I can attest to this each day I spend in my incredible home and see my family, the animals, and all of nature in beautiful harmony.

I didn't grow up with this kind of tranquility. There are days the chaos tries to return, but I work hard every day to maintain serenity in my inner life here on Earth. If I did not find this truth within myself, I wouldn't be able to help the people who come to me seeking their own peace and a sense of closure to their grief and loss.

Finding a Way to Forgive

Forgiveness is the third key, and I know that I could not have fully grasped the truths of love or peace without mastering forgiveness. If we believe that there are no bad guys and that we pick our life lessons in order for our souls to evolve, then it follows that we must also forgive wrongdoings against us. We chose our circumstances in order to learn, so instead of feeling hate or anger, we could instead choose to be thankful—thankful for the lessons we learned and the experiences that allowed us to grow.

This might seem like a stretch to you now, and that's okay. As you travel through my journey with me, you may think I would have found forgiveness impossible. But I'm here to tell you that no, it is not. I truly believe that my experiences with my abusive father and ex-husband are why I am where I am today. They were brave souls indeed for following through with the promises they made to my Spirit and for ultimately teaching me what I needed to know. Forgiving them took many years, and it wasn't easy. But in the end, I felt such a sense of release. Then I realized I had an even bigger challenge: forgiving myself.

Forgiving oneself can be one of the most difficult things for a person to do; it certainly was for me. We might extend more kindness to a friend than to our own selves. Even after I began developing my ability as a psychic medium, owning my birthright, being proud of the healing messages I was giving, I still struggled to forgive myself for the choices I had made in the past. I struggled to find any tiny speck of real peace or true love for myself because I had made monumentally bad decisions along the way.

That is when I had to delve deeper into the truth of *forgiveness*. It was truly eye opening to learn that just as I had chosen people to teach me lessons in this life, others had chosen *me* to teach *them* as well. It's a two-way street. This meant that, at times, I had to be the "bad guy" in someone's story. *Wow,* I thought, when I first grasped this concept. *This explains a lot.*

I'm not using this concept as justification for my actions as right or excusing anyone for what they did. But I am explaining why it is so important to allow forgiveness to enter a situation. We'll delve into this complicated premise more in the telling of my own story. However, suffice it to say that once I had more perspective, I made better decisions as I was no longer punishing myself. I'm still not perfect every time, but definitely better.

Bringing Life into Balance

Once I achieved the freedom that comes with forgiving yourself, it allowed me to work on the final truth: balance. I continue to work on it daily. It's one of the most valuable lessons I share with family, friends, clients, and workshop participants.

Think about all the things most of us are juggling in our daily lives. We balance our work and personal lives, our diet, our checkbook. We strive not only for growth, but also to just feel right. If we teeter too far one way or the other, we might "drop the ball" or just feel "off" that day.

It's possible to have too much of just about anything: too much religion, too much chocolate, too much alcohol, too much greed, too much shopping, too much exercise. You can even have "too healthy" of a lifestyle, if you deny yourself anything and everything indulgent in pursuit of perfection—that's not balanced either. You get the idea. Chocolate and I still duel this one out from time to time, but just knowing that I need to have balance allows me to be aware of where I am and what I need to do to become realigned.

When I feel myself losing balance, it's like an alarm going off in my head, warning me that I've lost a bit of myself. The core of what we must learn is how important balance is: what it really means, the reason we need it, and how we can truly apply it in our lives. My ultimate hope is that, when we come to the end of my story, you will understand a lot more about balance.

Living Your Authentic Self: It's Crowded in the Closet

As you continue to practice love, peace, forgiveness, and balance in your daily life, you will begin to find your authentic self again. It isn't easy, but it's worth doing!

Your authentic self is the truth of your divine Spirit. It is who you were meant to be when you were born on this planet. I believe we are all born as our authentic selves, but we change and move away from this state as the world leaves its impressions on us. This person can emerge again when you practice and begin to master your own four truths.

As we embark on my own complicated journey, reliving the good and the bad that led to my life as a mother, a medium, a teacher, an author, and a reality-TV personality, you'll see how I lost my authentic self and how hard I struggled with all four of these truths. It's not pretty. I spent 30 years thinking I was completely crazy, and to make up for that craziness I would do anything and everything to try to fit in. This included telling lies to myself and others, and living in a very small world, one where my authentic self was locked tightly in a closet, hidden away from everyone.

Look around and you'll see that today people can be in the closet for a lot of different reasons. I really identify with all of them. For example, we probably all know members of the LGBTQ community who are struggling to free themselves and live their truth. We know that people are hiding things in the closet related to weight and eating disorders. Addicts are in the closet about their addictions, and anyone who feels different about any aspect of themselves is in there, too. It's an awfully crowded closet.

We hide our authentic selves because we don't want to disappoint other people or hurt them in any way. But the truth is that we do more damage by trying to not hurt others than if we just stood up and said, "This is who I am." It's really our lies that create the pain within others and, ultimately, the pain within ourselves.

But there is no need for us to be ashamed of who we are. We are on this Earth to discover our authentic self and display it proudly to the world, letting our light shine. I believe with all my heart that the four truths will help you do it. Know that this is your birthright, and it is still within you.

Through sharing my journey, I hope that you will recognize that it is not unique; although perhaps the outcome, speaking with dead people for a living, *is* a bit unusual! My message to the world is this: If *I* could overcome the debilitating shame, abuse, pain, and chaos that I have lived through, then *anybody can do it.*

In my darkest hours—and I had some very dark ones—I never thought I could find the kind of personal fulfillment I have found. Yet my life has become more than I could have possibly imagined; each day, it just keeps on expanding and deepening in meaning. I continually meet courageous people who tell me about the suffering they endured, and they admit to me that they felt and thought so many of the same things I did. It is how I know that I am not alone—and neither are you.

Now that I have accepted my truth and my ability to communicate with Spirits, I've unveiled my authentic self and am living my life purpose. I know with certainty that I am here to teach others to find their authentic selves and live their truths. I have found within myself a resounding voice about our inherent abilities to connect with the Other Side, and as I move forward on this journey my voice only gets louder. (But don't worry, you can always turn your TV down if it gets *too* loud!)

For me, whether I am quiet, loud, or in between, gratitude is the most powerful prayer I know of. I spend my daily life looking for new things to be grateful for. You can't be angry and grateful at the same time, so in order to find your truths, you must also practice being thankful for what you do have.

I am eternally grateful to be able to share my story of anguish and triumph. I trust that within it, you will find the tools to unlock your own truths.

Chapter One

THE PEOPLE IN MY BODY

It's ironic that it took me 30-odd years to acknowledge the existence of Spirits when, in fact, my very first memory as a child was of complete acceptance of these entertaining playthings that hovered around me.

I was about five years old, and my mom had just put me down for a nap. I remember that afternoon clearly, not only the sequence of events but also the way I felt as she lay me down—which was *not* okay. I was adamant: Kindergarteners *do not* nap, and I told my mom so all the way to my room. Refusing to sleep, I lay there with my tired eyes, staring at the white bull-shaped teddy that my older brother had won for me at a fair a few days prior. I was reliving the fun-filled day I'd had at the fair with my siblings, and I could still taste how good the cotton candy was—oh, and the corn dogs! How I loved corn dogs.

Suddenly a light caught my eye as it came down from the ceiling. It began as a flicker but grew and grew until it was a brilliant white that hovered right above my stuffed toy. One by one, more and more lights appeared. I wasn't sure what to think. I wasn't afraid but curious and intrigued by what was happening. The one thing I knew for sure: *This sure beats naptime!*

Before I knew it, the lights began to grow, morphing into different person-like shapes and dancing playfully around my room. I can't remember exactly how it happened, but I began speaking to the lights one by one as they started to take form. The lights didn't have faces, but they did resemble the outlines of bodies, so I began to consider them people just like me.

Although I couldn't hear their voices the same way I could hear my family speaking or the TV in the other room, I felt as if we were having a conversation. "Hello," I said to one, "Hey there!" to another, yet I was alone in my room. As more lights appeared, I greeted the new lights as well. "Oh, hi! You're coming, too?" I spoke as if they were people that I had already met, or at least people I was interested in knowing.

As the lights filled my room, they began to come closer and closer to me, until they passed right through me. It was as if they were going to come right into my body, but instead they passed through to the other side of me. I could feel them behind me. It sounded like a group of people surrounding me, just out of sight, whispering in my ears.

Once they passed behind me, I could no longer see them even if I turned my head as quick as I could to try to catch them. I knew they were all still there. I could hear and feel their presence, but I could no longer see all of them. *This is cool,* I thought at one point, realizing how special this sensation was. The most important thing I remember from that day was that I didn't feel weird or crazy, and there was no shame—if only that feeling could have stayed with me!

At one point, each of the lights had managed to move behind me, and try as I might I just couldn't see them. They were behind me long enough for my five-year-old attention span to lose interest, and I decided to get up and head to the door. So much had happened in that short time that I was convinced my mom had forgotten to wake me up. Naptime was surely over by now.

I rubbed my eyes and yawned as I walked out to the living room to see my mom. "I had a bigggg sleep," I said, mouth wide open, hoping I could fake my mom out. I wish! Instead, my mother didn't even need to look at the clock—her soaps had only just started, and even if kindergarteners don't nap, I knew the rules: "Mom needs some quiet time, too!" My mother got up with a huff of impatience and marched me right back to my room, listing all the reasons why five-year-old girls still *do* need naps.

Protesting every step down the hallway, I finally told her about the lights. "There were these lights that came down over my bull teddy. They talked to me and danced around the room all together—"

"Listen!" my mom interrupted. "There's no one talking to you in your room, and there are no lights on. You are being absolutely ridiculous." She firmly took me back to bed, but I didn't think it was ridiculous at the time.

"Well, I'm *not* lying," I mumbled to myself, realizing it was no use trying to convince my mom.

I didn't know it, but I had just experienced for the first time the three things that would go on to control virtually all of my young adult life: *lies, shame, and Spirits.*

Understanding Spirits and the Other Side

Looking back now, I know that those lights were Spirits. In fact, I still see Spirits today in a form similar to those dancing lights from that afternoon, and I've now developed my ability to communicate with them. While accepting their existence took me a long, long time, in that first moment with them as a five-year-old, I didn't know anything *but* pure acceptance. Of course, I didn't know exactly *what* I was accepting. I certainly didn't know that the lights were Spirits. They were still with me when my mom tucked me back into bed, so I kept talking to them. I was bored and still fighting my nap, and what else was there to do?

Was I using my imagination in this moment? Definitely. I believe that as human beings here on Earth, our mediumship abilities work through our imaginations. As children, our minds are untainted and free to take us into new, unknown worlds that exist only to ourselves. Our ego is not yet formed, so we have nothing to get in our way of this pure imagination, no judgment or critique of it. Even as adults, once we get out of our own way and look past our ego's preconceived ideas of how things are or should be, we can continue to use our imaginations to communicate with the Other Side.

For those who aren't familiar with how Spirits and the Other Side work, I usually explain this reality in the following way. You see, before we come into this world to play the "game of life," we are divine spiritual beings—what some may call *souls*. Personally, I prefer to use the term *Spirits*. As Spirits, we have a personality, likes and dislikes, and we are who we are; we are our authentic selves.

On the Other Side, our Spirit picks a body and chooses what gender we will be. This is our vehicle, our "host" if you will, while we are on Earth as a human being. The vehicle's job is to hold our Spirit for this part of our journey. When we cross back over to the Other Side (that is to say, when we die), we lose only our physical body. Our Spirit is made up of energy, and it remains. Our energy can indeed remain around our loved ones after the death of our physical body; they simply will not be able to see us in the same way after we pass over.

It's not just our loved ones, however, who are on the Other Side. There are also other Spirits whom we may not have known during their journey on Earth, but they help guide us toward our ultimate goals. *Guides* are Spirits who have experienced many lives on Earth and have learned all the lessons they came here to learn. They are "masters of life"—we may associate them with religious entities such as Buddha or Jesus. *Angels,* on the other hand, have never lived with us here on this side, but they often appear to us in the form of an animal or a person, or a thought in our head, to help us achieve our mission—to help us find our truths.

Angels and Guides help us with our life lessons and steer us in the right direction. But just like the Spirits of our loved ones who have passed, Angels and Guides can also communicate through our imagination. After all, everything on the Other Side is the same—it's all energy and we are all energy. And all of that energy is available to guide us on our way to find the four truths.

Our connection to the Other Side is particularly strong when we are children, because as children, we don't judge or question what we perceive. We merely watch, we listen, and most importantly, we believe—just like I did when I saw the lights dance around my room. This was a pivotal experience for me, but I had no idea of its importance until decades later. If only I had known at the time that I was seeing a gateway to knowledge, healing, and helping—what a different path my life would have taken.

Making Sense with My Childlike Mind

After my mother closed the door and put me down for a second round of naptime, sleep was far from my mind. I had so many other plans circling my head. I was going to figure out what was up with these lights and why they were hanging around. I began to talk to them, and I heard them as they talked back. They continued to move and dance around freely behind me, just out of my direct line of sight.

Suddenly, I had a great idea! What if they could help run my body? I'm a genius! I decided that the lights could stay and, as a five-year-old control freak, gave each one of them a job. I figured that since all of my other body parts had jobs, perhaps those old parts needed a break, having worked so hard for five years straight!

I figured that the light I had known the longest, the first to appear, should be put in charge of my right arm, as it was the one I used most. Another one I gave control of my left arm. One I gave to my stomach, another my legs, and others took on roles in my head, shoulders, hands, and feet. Collectively, I came to know them as the People in my body.

They were like a bunch of imaginary friends with jobs—the best kind! I kept them with me wherever I went, and they controlled my body whenever I needed them. If I was running to the washroom and not quite sure whether I would make it, I'd ask the person controlling my stomach to help me hold it in. *Push the button! Push the button!* I yelled in my head. If it were an emergency, I'd yell out loud to make sure the People would hear. When I was in class and didn't know an answer, I'd ask the People to give it to me. If I got it wrong, I just figured the People were mad at me or maybe they hadn't studied either.

Not long after I met the People in my body, Nana—my great-grandmother—passed away. I remember sitting on the floor of the living room of my grandma's house as my mom, aunty, and grandma decided what to do with all of Nana's belongings. I was bored and restless but too young to help, so while everyone was hard at work sorting through all the boxes and bags, I played with the People in my body and pushed my brother's dinky cars along the patterns of the carpet.

Then I saw my grandma lift a brightly colored tin box from the heap of Nana's personal items, and my eyes lit up. I saw her place the gold and red tin box on a table, and I admired it quietly. That gleaming treasure box was filled with enough costume jewelry to keep me busy for hours! I couldn't take my eyes off of it. I wanted so badly to play with it and keep it as my own, but I was much too shy and quiet as a child to ask for it myself. Maybe the People in my body could help?

I had come to rely on them as I would my best friends. Sometimes asking them to do things worked and sometimes it didn't; but in my mind, they helped make things possible. Naturally, it seemed like a good time to call on them right then, and I begged them to make Grandma offer me the box. I kept concentrating on my inner plea: "Come on, People. Please, please, please have Grandma give it to me!"

Only a few moments later, as if by magic, Grandma picked up the box and brought it to me. "Here, Lolly," she said, using my childhood nickname. "Would you like this box of Nana's jewelry?"

"Yes!" I screamed, probably a little too enthusiastically. Thanks again, People!

Growing Up and Away from Spirit

As I've said, I would talk to the People, and they would always talk back. Their responses would come to me in my head. We discussed life, my body, their work, and all the things that were going on in my life. Sometimes I would ask them to help me make friends. Sometimes I would just ask them to make sure my mom made my favorite lunch. (Campbell's tomato soup with Ichiban noodles in it—yum!) I'd beg them to move my legs fast enough to get home in time for the beginning of *The Flintstones* cartoons, because I hated when I missed the beginning. They were my go-to People.

For two or three years I did everything with the People in my body. In a real world where I struggled to fit in, one in which I struggled to make healthy human connections, these were *my People*—until I learned to experience shame.

When I was about eight years old, I began to realize that the People in my body didn't seem to be in anyone else's body. No one talked about having them, and I never seemed to catch others around me talking to their People. When I was caught talking to my People, I was told that they were made up or not really there. I was made to feel like I was different or weird. It didn't take long for me to learn that I should whisper when I spoke to my People, and soon all of my conversations with them were taking place only in my head.

I understood that it wasn't normal to have these People, but I didn't ever doubt that they were real. What I came to doubt was my ability to convince anyone else of their existence. In the same way that a toddler might ask their mom to stop setting a place for their imaginary friend at the dinner table (even though they were convinced that "Bob" was still there), I decided to pretend my People had moved on. Perhaps we all have People as small children, but at some point or another, we close off and conform to the norms of our society. In doing so, we deny our imagination, and we deny our truth.

When I was about 12, I started to let the People go altogether. I decided that they would need to find a new stomach, arms, and legs to control if I ever wanted to achieve a semi-normal life. I know now that this was my ego arguing with me, judging me, and making me get rid of them. Along with the People, a part of myself had to go, too. That's the part I searched for, for nearly 30 years after.

There was no way for me to know as a little girl that this ability I had to communicate with these People would eventually allow me to influence the lives of countless others. But before I could help anyone else through their misery, I first had to experience it myself. I had to get through my own complicated maturity process. I had to live through years of self-doubt, self-loathing, lies, shame, fear, anxiety, and abuse—and that reality began within the walls of my childhood home.

Chapter Two

LIES OF SHAME

I remember the first lie I ever told out of shame. It's the type of lie that pulls you away from your authentic self and pushes you further into the closet. I call these, simply, *lies of shame*. But let's not be too dramatic—we all do it.

On this occasion, I was in the third grade, walking home from school with my two friends, Mary and Beth. I was deeply envious of Mary. She had long, straight, shiny hair; my hair was curly and cut so short that it poked out in all directions. I was tall and gawky looking, a far cry from the image of perfect femininity I had in my head, of long blonde hair and lean legs. I wanted deep down to be an athlete, but I had no coordination and I really hated to run. (Come to think of it, I *still* don't like running!)

My envy of my friends was rooted deeper than just hair. Mary was being raised by a single mother, and because of the way my home life was, I'd come to believe that a family without a father was probably an ideal one. Even Beth's father was hardly ever around, because he traveled so often for work. She said that when he did come home, it was like Christmas! The house was filled with presents and love, which was inconceivable to me. I imagined that there was no drinking or yelling in *their* homes. I pictured what it would feel like to live somewhere with no tension, fear, or stress—and most importantly, no *shame*.

As the three of us walked together, Beth described the cookies she was going to bake with her mom when she got home. My jealousy grew and grew. In my third-grade mind, Beth and Mary had

THE TRUTH OF SPIRITS

it made. I felt their happiness and pride as they talked about all the great things waiting for them at home, while I became increasingly aware of the possibility of chaos awaiting *me*. Beth and Mary took light, quick steps toward their fatherless homes, while I dragged my feet as slow as I could. I dreaded seeing my father. Would he be drinking again? Would he be angry and yelling? Would there be a fight? Or worse, would we be moving? Not another move. *Please not another move,* I silently prayed.

I struggled to match my friends' excitement, but all I felt was shame, followed naturally by an extra-large side dish of disappointment. I wanted to be liked, as most children do, so I blurted out the most impressive story that I could think of at age eight.

"My mother is the queen of England!" I announced proudly.

The Power of Fantasy and Reality

Yes, my story was quite a stretch; but I figured if I was going to lie, I might as well go all the way! I was too young to even begin to understand how ridiculous it sounded. Reflecting on my lie of shame now, I know that it was based on a deep desire for what my friends had. At the time, I imagined that these two girls were as good as royalty.

Mary and Beth had no reason to suspect that my home life differed from their own. On the contrary, they probably had the impression that *my* family was perfect. To the outside world, my father could seem incredibly charismatic. He made friends with everyone, even NHL players—and for those who don't know, hockey is a *big deal* in the cold, white north of Canada.

My father owned several construction companies so we had to go where the work was, which meant that we moved at least once a year to new towns in the western provinces of British Columbia and Alberta. Uprooting our home and losing our friends so often was extremely difficult on me and my siblings, although my parents managed to construct new social circles with little difficulty. It seemed like we were always having gatherings and events at our immaculate home, especially during the holiday season. From the outside looking in, we seemed like the picture-perfect family.

"My mother is Queen Victoria, and I am the princess," I explained to Mary and Beth. "We are here on holiday, hiding out in Red Deer, Alberta, as a break from all that royalty stuff." I kept my back straight and tall the way I imagined a princess would stand. Surely they would believe my mother and I were truly on sabbatical from the castle, undercover in rural Canada, in a small farming town that any royal family would love to visit. *Not really, just kidding.*

I kept on divulging more information about my "secret life." My mother, I said, was so stressed from all the work of being a queen that we simply needed a break. Despite my friends' initial mistrust, I kept going about it until I finally had them convinced that it just might be true. My older brother Kevin, only a few paces in front of us, thankfully refrained from bursting my royal bubble and kept his smirk to himself.

By the time I neared the end of my walk with Mary and Beth, my lie had become much more powerful. I was feeling something I had never felt before. As their eyes grew wider, and their blatant disbelief morphed into a yearning to believe, *I felt accepted.* These girls were actually envious of me! My lie gave me a glimmer of hope; maybe I could hide the deep shame I felt about my own my home, as well as my body and my mind. I had a shot at being special—or, at least, *appearing* that way. And I'd learned from my parents that appearances were just as important as the real thing, if not more so.

When I had to separate from my friends and head down the street to my house, I began to pray. Please don't let my father be home and, oh, I hoped that my sister would let me play her piano. As I walked through the entrance, my brother Kevin gave my frizz-ball hair a sharp tug as he walked past me, his evil grin letting me know what he was about to do.

Of course, my sister did *not* let me play her piano, and to make matters worse, soon my entire family knew about my royal lie. (Thanks, Kevin!) The truth didn't take long to reach back to my friends either. Tears welled up in my eyes and I felt exposed as a liar, shot right back down to my low, far-from-special self. But what I remembered most vividly was that high before the low.

I remember that first lie the way you might remember your first experience with alcohol. It was my first taste of something *wrong* that made me feel so *right*. The feeling of being special was intoxicating, exciting, and powerful. Even though I got smacked back down to earth, like the hangover that comes after a drinking binge, that initial feeling of greatness was enough to make me want to try it again. I didn't exactly make it a habit to lie, though, and I never meant to be hurtful or deceitful. At the time, I truly believed that this was my only escape from all the shame that I had in my life.

The Roots of Shame and Fear

My early years were steeped in shame, but it wasn't always that way. There was a time when our home was full of smiles, love, and laughter. At least, that was the way I remember it.

The first house I lived in was beautiful. We lived on, believe it or not, Happy Valley Road. Perched on a lush, serene acreage on Vancouver Island in British Columbia, our home had tennis courts, tree houses, horses, and motorbikes—you name it, we had it.

Apple and peach trees lined our trim and orderly property. I still get taken back to this time of my life with every bite of a ripe and juicy peach. I remember peach picking with my grandpa as if it was yesterday. He used to climb so gracefully up the rickety wooden ladder that we were forbidden from playing on and hand down one peach at a time for us to place gently in the baskets. Heaven forbid we drop even one of my grandpa's prized peaches, or squeeze one too hard! "A bruised peach makes bruised jam," he'd say.

When I was almost six, however, some kind of financial burden fell upon the business that my dad owned, something I was much too young to understand. My dad was a stubborn man, and he felt a move to Alberta would allow him to rebuild his empire once more. However, that never quite happened, at least not as I recall it. It's hard to go backward from success and remember what it's like to live within more modest means.

Up until this point, from what I can remember, things in my home seemed fairly stable. Yet there was always an undercurrent of anger and upset with my father, and I even remember feeling fearful at times. I suppose when we were financially stable, it helped to buffer my family to some extent, but once the money was gone, the stress between my parents increased dramatically and, with it, so did our fear of his outbursts.

With the business in upheaval and the bills piling up, we packed up and moved away before I even knew what was going on. That's probably the beginning of the chaos. We moved away in a whirlwind, away from the tennis courts and peach trees, but my dad still managed somehow to keep up appearances. No one on the outside would have guessed the truth. We moved almost every year of my life from that point on. While each house was never as elaborate as the first, we still maintained an outward semblance of wealth, success, and some form of happiness—happy and affluent on the outside, broken and chaotic within.

My parents were so skilled at putting on a good front. No one ever saw through their elaborate lies of shame, although perhaps they were in denial even to themselves about the existence of any trouble. Perhaps they just chose to live in blissful ignorance of their own lives crumbling around them.

The Tapping of Chaos

My mother struggled to keep up with my dad's mood swings. I know she struggled in the marriage and tried very hard to stay and make it work. She loved my father, but I imagine his drinking and bad temper would just get to be too much even for her. Every so often, she would just pack us all up and leave, determined to stand on her own two feet and raise the six of us kids by herself. We would take the 12-hour drive back to my grandma's place more times than I could count; one year, we did so three times. I'm sure my older siblings understood the real reason for our impromptu trips, but I was ignorant of the full depth of my parents' difficulties. What I did know was that my father could blow up at any moment, and I learned to live in a state of constant fear and anxiety.

I realize now that, even before I was born, alcohol had become my dad's vice. He abused both alcohol and drugs, which led to physical and emotional abuse in our home. Being the youngest and, for a while, my dad's favorite, I was spared the torment my dad dealt out to my mom and siblings. Although I didn't know the reason for the tension in the house, I always *felt* it. That tension always surrounded me, and I refer to it now as the *tapping of chaos*.

I think the tapping was there even on Happy Valley Road. It was a nagging sensation that told me that chaos was just around the corner—*tap . . . tap . . . tap. . . .* Imagine what this constant tapping can make you feel like. Try it. Put this book down for a moment, then take your finger and gently tap the top of your hand. Just tap, tap, tap; keep tapping, over and over. Keep doing it while you read until it annoys you, and then keep going even though it's annoying. Eventually you'll become so used to it that you won't even notice it—that is, until you stop.

Now imagine that you were born to this kind of sensation. It's something that may get annoying and it may not feel quite right, but it's something you have always known. If it were to stop, you'd feel lost and confused. You'd begin to search for a way to re-create it because it's just so strange to be without it. Even though it's dysfunctional, you just don't feel right. Something is off. So you seek out the familiar.

I had become so used to this tapping of chaos in my life that it was almost like a safety blanket to me. It was the one constant in my life that, as weird as it sounds, made me *feel like me.* My dad's drinking and fighting, the moving and the tension, the shame and lies, it all reinforced this tapping. I learned to keep that chaos in my life because I thought that the tapping was what made me complete.

Addicted to the Tapping

I think that my mother must have felt the pull of that tapping, because we never stayed long at Grandma's—a couple weeks, maybe a month. My father would quit drinking, he'd tell her he was turning things around. And each time, my mom would pack us all up again and drive us back home to the tapping.

My father was a businessman who lived for the pursuit of success and measured his value by money. With money came power, and my dad wielded both. Because he saw financial stature as a sign of self-worth, he was also the most generous person I knew. He would give you the shirt off his back. But at the same time, if you crossed him, he could rip the shirt right off *your* back.

On top of all this, my father tied love to money. He worked so hard to love us with money, and I think he began to believe the two things were truly one and the same. He would hand us cash as we walked out the door, and if I had a friend over, he'd hand us each a 20-dollar bill and tell us to go get ourselves some candy at the corner store. (We were in *heaven*. Forty dollars bought a lot of candy!) As a little girl, I couldn't have fathomed at what price this luxury came; besides, I had a sweet tooth, and sugar was (and still is) my weakness.

To my father, money forgave hurt, it forgave abuse, and it forgave his addictions. At the same time, his love of money was the underlying reason for all the pain in the first place. I didn't realize the pressure my father put on himself to always appear wealthy and generous, even when he couldn't afford to do so. The pressure he put on himself created stress, which contributed to his drinking problem, which would cause his business to slip even further into failure, which increased his level of anger. We were always waiting for the next big outburst. *Tap . . . tap . . . tap. . . .*

I'm not sure exactly when my father's drinking and addictions reached a tipping point. I've heard my mother say that things really went downhill after my father had an accident and broke his hip while inspecting a job. He had to stop working while he recovered, and he was never the same after that. Medication and alcohol controlled his pain, but his frustration over the lost revenue and loss of pride led to years of self-destruction for him—and no end to the tapping for us. He was completely volatile, and anything or nothing might set him off.

I don't use my dad's past as justification for the events that follow. I believe that everything happens in our lives for a reason, and therefore requires no justification. However, analyzing my father's path helps me to understand my own journey. I believe that we choose the parents we are born to for what they can teach us, and I can now look back on the lessons my dad taught me with gratitude, rather than hatred or anger. I'd always struggled between feelings of love and anger for my father because of the chaos he brought into my life, for teaching me to yearn for the tapping. Now I know that it's because of him that I was able to keep my intuition so strong. And for that, I am eternally grateful to him.

The Power of Your Own Intuition

I believe that to be intuitive is our birthright. Our "sixth sense," as it is often called, was given to us to allow us to receive guidance. It is like having your own internal navigational system that tells you yes or no. It tells you to keep going or to stop or that there's danger up ahead. This inner intuitive voice is more than just a hunch or an inkling. It's actually guidance from our Guides, Angels, and Spirits, which are always around us. To tap into this guidance, we have to tap into the energy around ourselves and around others—what many people refer to as an aura.

Some people are naturally more attuned to this energy, just like some of us are better than others at skiing or art. Any of us could throw on some skis and fly down the hill, and everyone has the ability to paint or draw; it's just that some of us start out better than others. However, with teaching and practice, we learn to develop our abilities to become masters. Intuition is no different from any other ability. Even if we are born with natural talent, we still have to practice to maintain our skills. If you don't use it, you almost forget how, but you can regain your ability with some practice.

I believe that we are all born with an inherent psychic ability, but around the age of 11 or 12, we tend to let go of it. As we begin to develop our ego and the world around us leaves more of an impression on us, we begin to believe that our intuition is simply a by-product of our imagination. We discount our sixth sense as unnecessary. The truth is that as teenagers we actually need it more than ever! It's a valuable tool we can use throughout our whole lives to keep ourselves safe, yet open to opportunities.

Children who live with constant chaos often need to rely on their intuition to protect themselves from the dysfunction, so it's not surprising to me that many great intuitives, psychics, and mediums came out of horrific childhoods. They needed to keep their intuition strong just to survive. Without the difficulties they experienced in their childhood, as I did, perhaps they would have followed the usual path and abandoned their birthright as they entered their teenage years. It's not a hard and fast rule (not all psychics come from terrible childhoods, and not all abused children keep their intuitive abilities), but it's something I feel to be true in my life.

So around that pivotal age of 11 or 12, I held on to my intuition like it was a life preserver that would save me from all this chaos. I always had to stay one step ahead of my father. Would he be home? Would he be mad? Would he blow up? Without my intuition, I would never have known what was around the corner. I'd never know whether to hide or go running into his arms.

Taking the Good with the Bad

I know now that life comes in ebbs and flows, highs and lows. Our ability to balance and be flexible, to anticipate, to dodge and weave when needed, it's all part of the experience of human life. We learned in our family to enjoy the good times, but to never really let our guard down completely.

So mixed in with the fear and chaos, there were Hallmark moments. We kids would put on skits at Christmas, we played and swam in pools, and my dad lovingly made outdoor skating rinks for us. I remember the way Santa never had time to wrap our presents, but we knew there would be a pile of them waiting for us on Christmas morning!

I think of the nights when my father would sneak me into the big bed and feed me chocolate chip cookies. I'd giggle while my mom searched madly for me so she could put me to bed. When she'd peek her head through the door and ask my dad if he'd seen me, he would throw the covers over my head and shrug his shoulders with bewilderment. Finally my mom would catch us—me, passed out asleep with chocolate all over my face, and my dad pretending he had nothing to do with it. I was his little girl, *his princess.*

Yes, there were happy moments among the chaos, yet the tapping remained a constant. I guess that explains why even some of my happy memories also trigger fear. We might be on top of the world one moment, but it would never last long. It was only a matter of time until my father's anger crept back; he'd always find something to be mad at, or perhaps because he'd just gone too long without a drink.

I have fond memories of our family trips to Ontario. Dad owned several racehorses, so we'd go and cheer for them. We even got to stand in the winner's circle when one of them won! But when I think of these times, I also remember my dad yelling in the barn at the racetrack. One of the racehorses went crazy with fear, and it started kicking and bucking. I remember crying, and I became terrified of horses because I thought that they were just as unpredictable as my father was. (Later in life, I had to work hard to overcome this fear.)

My father was a man who could be incredibly gentle one minute and a complete tyrant the next, so it felt as if our home had a mood of its own. When my father was away, our home breathed easy; my mom smiled more and our hearts seemed lighter. When he was home, or even in anticipation of his return, the house became tight and still. It felt like there was an elastic band wrapped tight around it, and we could hardly catch a breath. Sure enough, that's when the tapping would intensify. It was warning me: chaos was coming.

For the Sake of the Family

As the youngest child, and my dad's only biological daughter, I had a special place in the family. Both of my parents had been married once before, and both of them had two children from their previous marriages—my dad had two boys and my mom two girls. There is a fairly big gap in age between me and those four oldest siblings. When my parents married, they had my older brother Kevin and then they had me, three years later. It was like the show *The Brady Bunch*, and I was the youngest girl, Cindy. But instead of the happiness that oozes from the TV set, we had the tapping.

My mother was fond of telling me how proud my dad was of having a girl. He carried around a case of champagne in the trunk of the car for weeks. After I was born, she said, he took me around to all of the pubs he visited regularly to show me off, and to keep me close. Because I was his first little girl, he rarely broke his temper with me, and certainly never physically gave me a reason to fear him. But there was a strange fear I could instinctively feel in my siblings and mother, which told me that something else was there and I needed to remain cautious.

I learned early on to take the good with the not so good in my young life. Because of the special treatment from my father, I often felt disconnected from my own mother. She knew my father spoiled me and not the other girls, and this made me different from my sisters. I know my mom loved me dearly, but I imagine she also resented the relative peace I lived in when she had to watch her other children suffer at the hands of this man who was their stepfather.

My mom kept a lot to herself and suffered in silence. I think she loved my father, but I believe she was also controlled by him and his money. She, like me, only managed to get as far as the ninth grade before leaving school, and she also started a family young. So my mother had limited financial and emotional capabilities to support six children on her own. Staying with your husband and making it work, regardless of the situation, is what women did at that time. And I must say, she did it well, putting up with a lot for the sake of us kids. The emotional and physical abuse was one thing, but the cheating took its toll on her, too, breaking her heart beyond repair.

When my mom did finally leave my dad for good, she was in her 50s, and she never let another man love her again. Maybe she was too broken to love again, or maybe she learned a lesson that took me years to learn: *loving yourself is far more important than any other relationship.* She learned one day, perhaps too late, that staying for the children doesn't make a marriage work.

For way too many years, I lived in the same way my mother did. I believed that making your marriage work was how you made your family work—and that you had to put both your husband and your kids before yourself. I came to believe that leaving was never the answer. A woman should bend like a thin twig and become everything her partner wanted her to be.

My mother and I both learned to hide the truth to live the life we thought the world expected us to live. We thought appearances were more important than truth, and so we each, in our own time, took ourselves further and further away from our own authentic selves.

For so many years, I chased the feeling of approval that had been so amazing to me when I told that monumental lie to my little friends on the way home from school. I chased that *wow* feeling for most of my adult life, just the way my mother did. As my lies of shame mounted, the scope of my lies grew with it.

But all I really wanted was for people to tell me that they loved me. I wanted to be told that I was good, that I was accepted for who I was. I searched for this validation on the outside, because I truly believed deep down that I could not love myself until *others* loved me. I chased that elusive acceptance so ruthlessly that it could have killed me—and it very nearly did.

Chapter Three

"I MUST BE CRAZY"

My heart was beating so loudly, I didn't even hear the clamor of noisy students filing into the classroom from outside. I tried to control my breathing so that no one could tell just how much discomfort I was in, but I could feel a million eyes looking down at me. Pain, confusion, and shame were building up within me, crawling under my skin; I was sure it must have been seeping out through my pores.

My palms were hot and leaving sweaty prints on my desk, so I shoved my hands between my knees hoping to hide them. I was convinced everyone was still staring at me, and I was too embarrassed to look up to see if they were. The glass walls of my tenth grade math class felt as if they were closing in around me.

As Mr. Thompson banged on the board to demand our attention, I did everything I could to avoid looking at him. I stared at the floor for a while, moving my glance from one student's sneakers to another, not even noticing that the class had begun.

I couldn't take the sound of my pounding heart anymore. As the beating expanded into my throat, I looked up, right at Mr. Thompson, and I heard it. I wasn't hearing voices outside my head, but rather hearing thoughts inside my mind. But these weren't *my* thoughts. I didn't have a clue *where* these thoughts were coming from, and I remember thinking: *I must be crazy.*

The Rippling of Fear

By the time I was 15 years old, sitting in Mr. Thompson's math class, I had all but forgotten about the People in my body. These thoughts that had suddenly intruded into my mind that day were very much like how the People used to communicate with me, but something had changed since then. This time my reaction was not one of acceptance, casual curiosity, or fun; this time I was terrified.

As the fear rippled through my body, anxiety did, too. My heart beat louder and louder as I tried with all my might to get those thoughts out of my head. Now I know that the fear was actually caused by my denial, my complete rejection of the thoughts. The anxiety I felt was a fight between the two sides—an internal fight between acceptance and rejection; between the truth of Spirits and the reality that society had forced upon me that whatever this was, it could not possibly be happening.

But in that moment, all I knew was I *must* be crazy—or maybe I had a brain tumor. How could this be happening to me? I could tell that no one else in class was hearing these voices because as I looked around the room, I saw the other kids laughing and talking. And somehow, strangely, I became aware that these weird thoughts were linked to our teacher.

Every time I looked at Mr. Thompson's face, a new thought would fly into my mind, interrupting what I was thinking. Soon I was unable to take my eyes off of his face; I could even feel what he was feeling. It's not as though I was reading his mind exactly, but whatever he was worried about, scared of, or angry over, seemed to be rippling into my head.

Then, all of a sudden, I could sense that he was about to explode. I also knew that it didn't really have to do with how unruly the students were being at the moment or that Jake was talking back to him as usual. I knew with certainty that Mr. Thompson hated his job and being in this classroom nearly as much as I did! He'd realized early in his career that he had no patience for teenagers, and now that his own kids were reaching that troublesome age, he regretted not taking action on this realization sooner. I also sensed that he hated the routine he was locked into. And he really hated the lunch his wife had packed for him that day—tuna salad, when she *knew* he hated tuna!

But why do I know he hates tuna? I wondered. *How could I possibly know all this?*

Feeling Surrounded

The class finally settled down, and as Mr. Thompson's glance passed over me I suddenly knew that he hated me, too. I looked down in shame, as if my knowing this was like stealing a secret straight out of his head. The beating of my heart then grew into my throat, and pounded against every inch of my skin.

I shifted my gaze over to Jake—the dirty-blond boy in front of me who simply never sat still. As he fidgeted with his pencil case, I understood at once why he chose to sit so close to me. He liked my friend Kate, but his feelings for me were the complete opposite. *He thinks I'm weird. Oh yes, and he hates me, too.*

My thoughts were flying back and forth between all the kids who thought I was weird and then back to my own thoughts. *I'm crazy. He hates me. I'm crazy. She thinks I'm ugly. I'm crazy. He thinks I'm crazy. I'm crazy. I'm crazy. I'm CRAZY.*

"I'm crazy" became my mantra, repeating over and over in my head for more than 20 years. It was my go-to phrase. I honestly thought I *must* be crazy because I couldn't fathom any other reality.

My thoughts were like a runaway train, and I couldn't take it any more. *I'm crazy . . . I'm crazy. . . .* Attempting to get away from it all, I turned and stared at the walls at the back of the class. But those walls were made of glass, and their transparency opened me up to yet *another* world of thoughts. A few students lingered in the hallway behind us, and instantly I was there with them, in their thoughts. I knew immediately what they were on about, who hated me, who just disliked me, and who thought I was plain weird. *I am weird. And crazy!*

I didn't know it at the time, but my ability to connect with Spirits is strongest when I look right at somebody. In that moment,

I was not only dealing with the 22 people in my own class and the teacher, but also everyone else in the school as they walked by the glass walls of our classroom.

Imagine what this felt like for me. Imagine listening to your iPod, and every time you looked at someone their iPod's music synced with yours. You could hear their music playing simultaneously with your own, just a few octaves higher. Then imagine being in a glass room full of people, with even more people walking by. The more people you look at, the louder the music gets, and the more muffled the words. That's how I felt; only there was no music, just thoughts. Scrambled thoughts, playing over and over on top of each other, and a heart beating out of control. I felt like I was in a pressure cooker about to burst.

But how did I know how all these people were feeling and what they were thinking? Why did I know so many things about them just by looking at them? Where were these thoughts and feelings coming from? Suddenly, I couldn't take it any longer. I raised my hand and asked to use the bathroom. I ran out and never looked back. In fact, I never again went back to that math class with Mr. Thompson.

The Walls Are Closing In

The word *anxiety* wasn't a common one when I was younger. People didn't talk about having it, they didn't discuss it on TV shows or read all about it on Wikipedia, and they certainly didn't think a child could have it. In ninth grade, I didn't even know the word existed. I now know, however, that what I felt that day in class, was a full-blown anxiety attack. I went on to struggle with it for years.

I believe that many of you reading this have likely experienced anxiety and know how horrible it can be. Maybe you didn't have the same feelings and voices I did, but something caused you to be stricken with fear, nervousness, and panic. That feeling of sudden terror, as your heart races and you suddenly want to crawl out of your own skin, is what the doctors call anxiety. But I think it's actually much more, and there may well be underlying reasons that the doctors don't know about.

I know now that my own anxiety was caused by Spirits who were trying to connect with me. The longer I denied that connection, the more intense my anxiety got, until I began to suffer from full-blown panic attacks for years. Debilitating anxiety slowly controlled my life; I felt like walls were closing in around me. I would feel claustrophobic and unable to breathe, but sometimes it was even worse.

The most common time for me to suffer an attack was in public, particularly whenever I would have to look people in the eye. So I learned to avoid crowded places, which meant classrooms as a teenager, and I most certainly didn't look into people's eyes. I was a teen who didn't belong. I spent my days skipping classes and smoking—and while to some of you that might sound as if I fit into high school just fine, believe me when I say I didn't.

To make the whole situation worse, just two years prior to this, my parents packed up what was left of the household and moved us from Leduc, Alberta, to the "big city" of Edmonton. The timing was fantastic: right when we had only just begun to make friends. Even though we hadn't moved far away in relative terms, to a teenager, Edmonton could have just as easily been a whole other planet. I was furious with my parents for taking me away from one of the few friends I'd been able to make, Jill.

My sister Tracy decided not to come with us and moved back to British Columbia instead, which was really hard on my mom. The two of them had grown incredibly close as a result of my dad's abuse, and Tracy was probably the only person who truly understood my mother—at least, that is how it seemed to me. The brother closest in age to me, Kevin, came with us for the move, but he was never really around. He got a car, which I was envious of because a car meant freedom. He even got to keep attending school in Leduc, and he was hardly ever home.

My oldest sister's daughter also made the move with us. She had come to live with us while we were still in Leduc, displacing me in my role as the youngest in the family. I was also certainly no longer the cutest, because she broke the rules for cuteness. Even though the pedestal my dad had put me on had been nearly razed since his addictions took over his life, it was now clear that my safety net of being his "little girl" wasn't going to protect me into my teenage years.

We were headed for a showdown. When you add the ever-present tapping into this volatile situation, and the fact that my rebellious teen attitude was intensifying at the same pace as my father's addictions, I could see that it wasn't going to be pretty.

"Boy Crazy"

I took on the title of "teenage terror" at full force, and I'm not sure my mom was prepared for what was coming. Maybe the previous five teens she'd raised numbed her emotionally, or she just hadn't been expecting the same from me. I could see from her worn-out face that she just couldn't take any more, but that didn't seem to change my behavior. I began to rebel, and I *really liked* boys.

Before life changed for me, that is to say, before I faced those glass walls and the onslaught of Mr. Thompson's thoughts, my life was like any other teen's—apart from the tapping. Despite not fitting in at school, I'd been able to stay friends with Jill, my best friend from Leduc. I'd even found a boyfriend, if I can go so far as to call him that.

He was my first real crush, and I met him while at a fair in Saskatchewan that my dad went to in search of new business partners. This boy's name was Brad, and he was one of the game operators. Jill and I spied him from afar, and finally built up the courage to speak to him. Brad was tall, lean, and handsome, and he looked at me differently than I'd ever been looked at by a guy before.

We played one game at his tent, which turned into an entire afternoon of talking and flirting, which turned into a week of hanging out with Brad at the fair. He was 20, so I told him I was 17, because I figured he wouldn't be interested in a 15-year-old. Sure enough, by the end of the week, I was twitterpated. I think he was smitten, too, at least enough to give me his number, which I guarded like gold.

At the time, Brad was traveling with the fair to earn money to go back to school, but once he got back to his home in Ontario, we were both glued to the phone. Hours and hours were spent in conversation, to the point where Brad was looking into jobs for me and we were planning my escape to Toronto to be together. He would send me songs about love, and tell me the lyrics reminded him of me. I'd giggle with Jill and blush on the other end of the line. I felt *special.* I thought that I loved him. It didn't hurt that he was extremely cute.

Looking back now, I know I wasn't ready to have a real relationship with anyone. I was too young to understand love, and I had a lot to learn about trust. The fact that I'd tried to build a relationship with somebody on a lie, naïve to the fact that I'd ever have to tell him the truth, speaks volumes on its own. Perhaps even more tragically than my ignorance of relationships and lies, was my ignorance about long-distance charges. That would come back to bite me in the ass—big time!

I'd seen my father talk on the phone with his relatives in Ontario hundreds of times, so I thought nothing of it. Too bad the phone company didn't agree. A few months into my long-distance telephone affair with Brad, the phone bill revealed *thousands* of dollars' worth of long-distance charges. All I can say is that I was lucky my father was out of town for business as the bills came. My mom may have been livid, but it was nothing compared to my dad's anger.

"What do you think you are doing?" she asked me, a sentence I'd come to loathe in the coming months. To be honest, I really didn't know the answer. I can still bring her tone to mind, as clear as the day she said it. Her voice was full of anger but fear and concern as well; I'm sure the concern was not just for my own well-being, but for hers, too.

How was she ever going to pay that bill? We were struggling financially as it was, and my dad seemed to "forget" to send any money at all. He had been spending more and more time in the U.S. on a new business venture he'd started up. While we enjoyed a reprieve from the chaos, he left my mom with the stress of keeping up appearances with a fraction of the money we used to have. My mom hadn't worked in years, and her previous jobs had usually been handling business matters for my dad's companies.

I know I added weight to my mom's shoulders. I felt bad, really I did; but don't forget, I was a teenager. So when my mom warned me, "You *need* to stop calling this boy!" I really only took it half to heart. I cut down on the number of calls, but didn't stop altogether. It seemed like those stolen moments were the only points of sanity in my life. I felt like I was someone else, someone normal, someone who wasn't living in an unhappy, abusive household.

But once I heard Mr. Thompson's thoughts and voices beyond the glass walls, I said good-bye to my normal teenage angst of boys and phone bills. I stepped into something far more debilitating.

A Lack of Focus

Grade 10 became a living hell. It became so difficult to force myself into any classroom without running out shortly after. I managed to skip the entire first month of school; everything after that first math class, in fact. I was terrified that the voices would take over my head again, so I just ditched all my classes.

I expect that the principal was unsure as to whether I was actually attending that school, so he gave my mom a call about two months into the year, asking her to come and discuss my lack of focus. Coming home from that meeting, I heard that dreaded line again. "What do you think you are doing?" she scolded me. "If you'd only apply yourself, Carmel; you're so smart but you just don't care."

I was lucky that it was only my mother lecturing me and my dad still had no clue about what was going on, but I was beginning to tune out her lectures. She sounded like a broken record, and it was easy for my thoughts to go elsewhere. I was trying to avoid facing the truth of what happened that day in math class, to ignore my mantra *(I'm crazy, I'm crazy, I'm—)*. I most certainly didn't want to admit to my mom the reason for why I wasn't going to class; they'd lock me up for sure!

I pledged that I would start going to school because I knew that's what my mom wanted to hear, but I never followed through with my promise. As much as I wanted to, I couldn't make myself walk through the door of those classrooms. Mom tried to make me, but it was like she'd run out of energy with me—or maybe with life in general. For the rest of the school year, I got up every day and got on the school bus, but to my horror, I discovered that nowhere was safe. The intrusive thoughts and feelings weren't quarantined to the classroom, they found me on the bus and in the hallways of the school.

Soon I was battling anxiety on a regular basis. Having to sit still seemed to make the feelings worse, especially in a crowd. I eventually figured out that when I kept moving and avoided groups, I felt less panic and anxiety. So I would walk right past my classroom door every day and go straight to the cafeteria. When it became crowded, I moved to another spot with fewer people. Moving around was my coping mechanism; wherever students were, I wasn't. It was like musical chairs.

While I avoided those weird feelings the very best I could, I didn't skip *every* class. I did not need another dreaded call to my home about my lack of focus. So I would pop into cosmetology class every now and then, but failed at learning much there. I couldn't even learn to braid hair. I mean, the way my frizzy mane was, it really just didn't seem possible. Foods class was okay because there was space to move around more. If I were having a good day, I'd sit in the back of my social studies class, which was taught by one of the teachers I seemed able to handle best—but good days in tenth grade were few and far between.

I thought my life could not get much worse . . . but I was wrong. The battle royal was in the works. Things were about to explode.

⚬ⓒ ⓢ⚬

Chapter Four

RUNAWAY

No matter what school I was transferred to, I was always seen as a bit different. I wasn't always thought of as "crazy," but I was always "the new kid." Soon I was just "the outcast." As a result, I became accustomed to hanging out with any kind of crowd—whoever would accept me.

Things were different in this school, though. My refusal to attend class meant I was hanging out with a whole new group of rebels. These were the students who also thought that attending class wasn't a top priority, who thought being "troubled" was actually something cool. For the first time I felt like I almost fit in. Even with my constant moving away from crowds, I was rarely alone. I'd sit at the cafeteria table or in the smoke pit, and it would never be more than a few minutes before I had someone to talk to. Generally it was just one or two people at once, which I'd learned to deal with. I'd also learned that I experienced less anxiety if I were around people I'd gotten to know. Although some folks affected me worse than others, I simply avoided them. It was nice being able to feel comfortable with a few friends and just be able to *focus.*

I've since come to understand that Spirits are around all of us, all the time. As a teenager, they knew I could hear them, so they kept trying to give me their messages to pass along. They grew more and more persistent, clamoring for my attention, even though I refused to acknowledge them or listen to them. Some people have stronger and more persistent Spirits around them than others, and some Spirits seem to be more forceful when passing on their messages. That was what was affecting my levels of anxiety, although I didn't know it at the time.

Looking back, I also know that my negative experiences were more strongly affected by the energy of the people around me than the Spirits who wanted to connect through me. I mean, not all kids in high school are surrounded by lots of loved ones who had died. In the end, it all comes down to *energy*. I've always been able to sense when others are talking about me or feeling negatively toward me. This was really hard for me as a young girl, and I often wished I didn't know. It took me many years to learn that it's none of my business what other people think about me. But right then, in high school, I just wanted to be cool.

Bad Choices

Into my third month of skipping class, I thought I finally knew what to do. My ticket to fitting in, I decided, would be to bring a large bottle of vodka to school. I had no intention of actually drinking it myself; I'd tried alcohol and still couldn't figure out why anyone would like something so gross. But I knew that accessing the well-stocked liquor cabinet at home could very well get me on the path to acceptance.

This time I didn't need to lie to anyone, I thought. I just needed to grab some vodka, no questions asked, right? Unfortunately, that short-lived idea crashed and burned when my mom, completely out of the blue, decided to check my bag before I went to school. Today, of all days—*really, Mom?* Although she's never claimed to be psychic, she's always had a keen intuition. In this particular situation, however, I think we were both wishing she hadn't been so sharp.

At the same time, I was almost as surprised as I was disappointed that my scheme had been uncovered. My mom and I had become so disconnected in recent months that I wasn't sure whether she even knew when I was home. Although my dad's absence meant our house breathed a bit easier, he'd left a heavy financial burden on my mom's shoulders. Money arrived from him infrequently, so my mom was forced to take a job at a nearby bowling alley. Our gas and power got turned off regularly. I remember her plugging into the neighbor's power at one point to keep our house just barely functioning.

First Brad and the phone bill, then skipping class, and now I was sneaking alcohol. I could have said the words for her before they even left her mouth. "What do you think you are doing?" she said, but this time her anger overshadowed the fear and concern. I couldn't blame her for her fury. Now that I'm a mother, I understand how the fear must have boiled up inside her with nowhere to go but anger. Sooner or later, she knew, my dad must find out. Sooner or later, there would be consequences she couldn't protect me from.

So, out of guilt for the disappointed look in my mother's eyes, I went to school that day—sans vodka. I tried my best for my mom, but as usual, I still couldn't focus. I'd given up and was sitting outside school having a smoke when a guy I'd never seen before sat next to me. He was tall and handsome, a clean-cut musician type. My parents would approve, I thought, at least at first glance.

We talked and he told me his name was Chase. When he left I realized that despite him looking me straight in the eyes, I didn't have those strange feelings I normally did. My heart didn't race even while he was around! I had to know more, and I grew close with Chase very quickly. My calls with Brad became even fewer and far between.

Chase came from a good family with morals and values. He was nothing like me. We didn't have much in common, but we got along swimmingly. Unlike most males, or most people for that matter, Chase made me feel safe. More than ever at this point in my life, I yearned to feel safe.

Not long after Chase and I had become friends, I awoke one day in a panic. Something inside me was screaming for safety, but I couldn't tell you what exactly was wrong. I just got on the bus to go to school as if it were any other day, but my thoughts suddenly fixated on my dad. He was coming home today; I could feel it. My mind raced to all the events he had missed, all the lectures my mom had given me in his place. I knew that mail was going to be coming very soon with a black-and-white record of how I haven't been going to class. Would that be today? Oh, and the new phone bill!

I wasn't sure I could keep hiding behind my mom for much longer. She'd been telling me that she was out of patience, that she'd had enough. When the bus stopped at the transit station, I'd already made my decision. I needed to get out of there. I ran to school and the minute I saw Chase, I blurted out, "I need to run away." I told him I was sick of the fear in my home, that I hated my parents, and that I was angry with my dad for his drinking. I listed a million reasons why I needed out. But Chase didn't need reasons; that's how he was, he didn't even ask questions. I needed help, so he would wrap me in his kindness and solve my problems.

Chase had a way of making everything feel just fine, even if my life was far from it. He contacted a friend to drive me to the mall in Leduc after school, where I arranged to meet my friend Jill. She said I could live with her awhile. With my problems now hidden beneath the safety blanket Chase wrapped around me, we giggled in the car on our way to Leduc, oblivious to what was going on at home. I was leaving all that behind in the rearview mirror of Chase's friend's Volkswagen Bug!

I shouldn't have been so casual. My mom was well aware that I had not come home, that I should have been home hours ago.

Dad was home.

No Way to Escape

Dad had come home hungover only to be greeted by a letter from my school as well as the new telephone bill. It was the highest bill yet; I'd racked up a total of $4,000 with my phone conversations to Brad that summer. Then there was my interim report card, which was just as wonderful as I'm sure you imagine it to be. My intuition may have told me to run away that day, but it should have known better and told me to run *even farther.*

34

I was standing at a pay phone at the mall, calling Jill to come get me, when my brother Kevin's truck pulled up. My mother was sitting next to him, and they waved for me to come over. Fear gripped the inside of my stomach. I didn't even think to run. I just bowed my head in resignation and walked toward them.

I could see that my mom wasn't angry, just completely defeated. "Carmel, what do you think you are doing?" Her voice was full of sadness. She knew she couldn't protect me anymore.

Not a word was spoken the entire ride home. When we walked through the door, the house's breathing felt stale and tense. No words needed to be said—I could feel in my stomach that my father was home. The stench of stale alcohol hit me, confirming my dread. As I tried to sneak inside, my niece came running out. "We're going to Chuck E. Cheese's!" she screamed excitedly. But I knew *I* wasn't included in that "we."

As my brother, mom, and niece walked out the door, I realized that my days of unbiased love from my father were now officially over. Kevin caught my eye just before he left and I knew that he wished, despite our disconnection, I had remained the white swan, the princess on the pedestal that Dad never got to.

Violence Ready to Explode

I stood by the kitchen sink, unsure of what was going to happen next. I was so nervous that I found myself drinking one glass of water after the next without stopping for air. I didn't know how to prepare, because I really had no idea how my dad was going to react.

My dad finally came down the stairs, his jeans held up by his biggest belt buckle. Sweat glistened off his bare chest, and I looked away from him in fear. He looked awful, and even from the other side of the room, I could smell the stale sweat and alcohol.

"So, you haven't been going to school?" His voice hit me, so loud and deep that the hairs on the back of my neck vibrated. There was a threat in his tone so chilling, my bladder let go. I was 15 and I had just wet myself, yet embarrassment was the furthest thing from my mind. Before I could muster up a reply, his hand hit the side of my head with such force that I flew to the ground, landing at the base of the cupboards.

He kicked and kicked and *kicked* at any part of me he could get at. He used such force that he grunted with every swing. I lay on the floor with my arms curled in an attempt to protect my head. I wasn't sure what else to do; I just held on as tight as I could. Surely he wouldn't kick me in the head?

Finally one of his kicks missed and his toe hit the bottom of the cupboard with a nasty bang. He howled in pain and the beating stopped, but the fury of his anger only intensified. He reached down and grabbed me, picking me up by the back of my shirt as if I were a rag doll. Too weak and stunned to protect myself, I barely moved as he walked me out of the kitchen and threw me headfirst into the front door. My vision blurred, my ears rang, and everything started to go black. I thought I was going to pass out and struggled to keep my head up.

Dad picked me up again to throw me at the stairs. He kicked my ass up every step as I stumbled my way to the top. I tried to move out to the way of his foot, but failed miserably. As he continued to whale on me at the top of the stairs, all I can remember feeling was a sense of disbelief. As strange as it might seem, I couldn't believe this was happening to me. While I knew deep down that my dad was capable of beating anyone to a pulp, that he'd done so to others, I hadn't been convinced he was capable of doing it to *me*.

We'd reached my parents' bedroom now, my body limp and tears pouring down my face. I think my father's intention at this point was to spank me; maybe that had been his intention all along before he'd lost control. He struggled to pull off his belt but gave up in frustration and grabbed me by the throat. He lifted me off the ground. I couldn't breathe; I was *choking*. He was yelling, but all I could hear was his heavy breathing and muffled voice as my vision blurred and my ears continued to ring. *This is it,* I thought. *I'm dying.*

Suddenly I felt hot and muggy air entering my throat as he let go. I gasped for a breath so desperately I think it even shocked my dad. He pointed his finger toward my room, still yelling words I couldn't begin to comprehend. I left as quickly as my feet would take me, so relieved to finally find safety.

I didn't even bother to remove my soiled pants as I climbed into bed, I just threw my covers over my head and let my tears stream onto the pillow. I cried and waited for sleep to take me away. Away from the tapping, away from my father, away from all the crazy thoughts that were not my own—anywhere but here.

Bruised and Broken

I hadn't been sleeping long when I heard my door creak open, jolting me awake with the fear of not knowing who it was. It was Kevin peering in, and by the way he looked at my face, I could tell that I didn't look good. I could feel a shiner starting to form on my right eye, and who knew what else. His voice was cold and angry, "I want to see you down in my room in two fucking minutes."

I had no fight left in me, nothing more to give. I quickly changed into my pajamas and headed downstairs in defeat. I felt helpless, yet angry. My brother was upset with me for being so stupid as to antagonize my dad, but he was also mad at himself for leaving me to face his wrath alone. While my mom and brother had known full well when they left that Dad was about to inflict a punishment, neither of them had fathomed that my father could ever be so harsh to me.

I didn't hear a word as Kevin yelled at me. I gathered up the little energy I had to mutter, "Shut up." In frustration, my brother grabbed my hands to get my attention, and I screamed in pain. (Later I'd discover that my dad had torn all the tendons in my hands and forearms.) Kevin's eyes revealed the sadness in his heart, which he was trying so hard to cover with his anger. Unable to deal with his guilt or my pain, Kevin sent me back to my room, and we never spoke of that day again.

Until I started writing this book, none of my family members had really known the full truth. That was the norm in our family;

we didn't talk about painful things. It was as if we felt that not talking about something meant that it simply hadn't happened. Or, at least, it would *appear* that way; and of course appearances were often all we had.

I don't remember seeing my father the morning after the beating, but my mom was sitting at the kitchen table when I came down for school. She stared at me long and hard; I could tell she was evaluating my injuries. Her eyes were filled with as much sadness and pain as my heart. I imagined that, whether it'd been his idea or hers, she was questioning her decision to leave me alone with my dad.

"You don't have to go to school today," she said. That was the only time she would reference that event.

But we all know that not talking about painful things doesn't mean they didn't happen. It just means we don't heal until we do acknowledge them. I was angry. I wanted to go to school so Chase could see what my dad had done to me. I wanted sympathy and someone to care. But I was too broken. So I did what I was told and went back up to my room, burying that anger deep in my heart, holding it there for a few more decades to come.

Picking Up the Pieces

I don't remember when life at home went back to normal. I guess to some extent, it never changed. The house was still tense and my dad's actions were never discussed, but something inside me changed that day. My normal chaos returned, and the tapping became stronger. The only person I felt safe enough to tell about that night was Chase. He offered to help me fix this problem just as he did the last, but we both knew there was no real fix.

I started attending more classes. I was more afraid of the consequences than the anxiety. I also stopped talking to Brad entirely, as Chase and I were growing even closer and I feared the outcome of another outrageous phone bill. I needed Chase's safety even more now, and I wanted to be around him as much as I could. Naturally, our friendship turned into something more, and he became my first serious boyfriend. He was the one person I could be myself with. When I was with him, I wasn't anxious and my heart didn't beat uncontrollably in my throat. I could share anything with him, and I did share everything. Well, except for my crazy thoughts.

I didn't know how to articulate what was going on, so I tried to hide it from everyone around me and even from myself. I refused to acknowledge the truth of the voices and the feelings I was experiencing. I was caught in the same cycle as my parents every time they moved, every time my dad drank. Hide the truth, grow the shame.

Soon, my parents were back to weaving their own lies again. Just as the school year came to an end, we were boxing up our things and moving back to British Columbia—where, my mom informed me, I would start working for my sister Tracy. They tore me away from Chase, the one place I felt safe; and at the same time, they tore me away from my childhood.

The Sister Sessions

My mom thought that I would be happy about working. "It will teach you responsibility about money," she said and referenced the hefty phone bill I'd racked up. She probably thought she was saving me from my dad as well, but I don't think she anticipated the aftershock effects of the quality time I would spend with my sister that summer.

As Tracy and I spent all day and night together for two months, she began opening up to me about her own childhood in the house of chaos. Tracy knew that I had been punished for my outrageous phone bill and lack of focus, but I don't think she ever really knew the extent of the beating. In my sister's world, I was still the "white swan" who never got to see the tyrant of a father they all lived with. I think Tracy wanted me to understand why such a big disconnect had grown between us. Still, I knew by the things she said every now and then that she still thought of me as the lucky one, and that my single beating was nothing compared to what the others had been through.

One day at work I wrote an order on my hand, unable to find a piece of paper, and Tracy nearly lost her mind. "Do you know what Dad did to me for writing on my hand once?" she asked, the fear in her voice nearly as strong as the anger. "He scrubbed my skin clean with water so hot he gave me *third-degree burns*."

I came to understand that Tracy was still healing from the pain my dad had caused her over the years. It was even clearer in the evenings after we'd finished work, and after Tracy had her third or fourth beer. Although she didn't know she was doing it, as the demons of her past with my dad resurfaced, she was fueling my own hatred toward him. Sitting in a recliner chair across from me, night after night, Tracy started a routine of sharing her pain, a routine that intensified the anger bubbling up inside me. Her stories made me hate my dad not only for the pain he caused me, but also for the pain he caused others.

Because my siblings had been so much older than me, I had no idea of the pain they'd endured before I was born. But one thing was for sure: my father was no longer a man in my mind, let alone my own father. To me, he had become a monster. My anger grew, and I knew in my heart that I could never go back to his home.

Night after night, as Tracy relived her pain, I made a plan. I would run away, and I'd make sure I never had to see him again. This time I'd stay away.

On the Run

For help, I turned again to my safety net, Chase. He promised to get me out, and together we hatched a plan. I was determined that this time, I wouldn't be brought back. When Chase arrived, we borrowed my mom's car and said we were headed to the movies. Instead, he drove me to the Greyhound station and put me on a bus to Edmonton.

I was free for now, but Chase still had to return my mom's car! "She wanted to leave here. She can't be here, and she can't be with you," he told my father as he pulled up to the house. My dad dragged Chase out of his seat and barked at Kevin to jump in. They hunted me down one station at a time. The entire 13-hour ride to Edmonton, I cowered in my seat. I had a sinking feeling that my father was just behind me. I felt my stomach clench at every stop, terrified that my dad would storm through the door and drag me back. At one point, I thought to myself, *What do I think I'm I doing?* But maybe that was just because I was so used to my mother asking me that.

My doubt lasted only a split second before it was overtaken by anger. I hated my father. I couldn't be anywhere near him. If I went back he would probably beat me again. And I knew beyond a shadow of a doubt, he would make me move again. There was no way they'd let me finish high school in the same town. All those promises they made were always lies. I had enough lies of my own; I had no room for theirs.

I didn't get a wink of sleep the entire bus ride, kept awake by the pain of fear and the extraordinarily strong tapping. I could almost feel my dad's belt—the one he'd struggled to get off—slamming across my skin. I imagined him yanking me off the bus and giving me a taste of what Tracy had known so well. I sat there wondering how my parents had reacted. Had Chase managed to break the news to my dad and escape unscathed?

While I replayed what might have happened in my head, I realized I had forgotten to pack my nana's jewelry box. That red and gold tin box that the People had helped me get was the one thing I'd managed to hang on to through all the moves. I had a bond with it that I couldn't quite explain. Perhaps it was a connection to my childhood that I felt, before the chaos, fear, and shame. A tear dripped down my face as I wondered whether I'd ever see my box or my family again.

When I finally reached Edmonton I was the last person to get off the bus. I was shaking scared. What if my dad had somehow gotten there before me and was waiting for me outside that door? But the only person I saw was my friend Kayla, whom I'd arranged to meet. Unbeknownst to me, my dad and brother had given up their hunt. I took a deep breath, the first I'd managed for the whole trip, and walked off the bus, hesitant but hopeful.

Craving Familiar Patterns

I could still sense the tapping, but I felt safe. I could feel my dad's grip on me slowly loosening. I didn't call home, and my parents never called me, not that they knew how to find me. I was free, free as a bird! Well, except for those intrusive thoughts that didn't belong to me.

I adjusted surprisingly easily to my newfound freedom. I lived with Kayla and her parents in a home that couldn't have been more different from my own. I was free to come and go as I pleased, to stay out as late as I wanted (within reason). The first few months, though, I feared my world would come crashing down. Dad's car would come roaring up to drag me back to his world, I was sure of it.

But as time passed, the tapping got lighter and lighter until there was none at all. I was free of the chaos I'd become so comfortable with my whole life. Yet its absence gnawed at me. As strange as it might sound, subconsciously I even began to miss it, to crave it.

I kept busy and tried to push the tapping—or rather, the lack thereof—out of my head. However, without it I felt out of place and uncomfortable in my own skin. I registered myself for school, partly to keep busy, partly because it was what I thought I was supposed to do, but it didn't go well for me that year. In fact, it was even worse than the first time I tried tenth grade.

I was frustrated with myself and my inability to go to class. I hated that I just couldn't focus, and I didn't know why I couldn't just power through it all. Still, I went to school every day, and hung out in the cafeteria or in the smoking pit. I was used to wanting to stay away from home anyway, and I wasn't sure what else to do if I weren't in school.

Then one day, while I was at my usual spot in the cafeteria, Kayla came running. She grabbed my hand and dragged me to the other side of the school. There was a new guy this year that I just *had* to see, she said. In our rush to his locker, we very nearly bumped into him! Although we usually completely disagreed on who was the hottest guy in the room, this time she was right. Paul was *very* attractive. Just, *wow.* Those were the days when Bon Jovi was *the* thing, and with his long hair and tight white jeans, this guy was *very* Bon Jovi.

Everything was going wonderfully for me. There was no chaos, no tapping—and that was the problem. There was no chaos with Chase, and now I had no chaos at home either. I was free, I was loved, I was safe. But despite my every effort to get away from the tapping, I didn't know how to navigate life without it. It made no sense, but I craved it. So when Paul started to flirt with me, what did I do?

I ran back to what I knew. I chose chaos over safety. I chose the comfort of the tapping. I chose Paul, and with it I chose what was to come. Every last painful second of it.

☜◎◉☞

Chapter Five

CHASING
THE TAPPING

Paul was a lot of firsts for me. He was the first man I truly loved, the first man I lived with, the first man I married. But mostly, he was my first major mistake. Don't get me wrong, he wasn't my only mistake—I wish!—but the *first* definitely has a way of holding on to you. The lessons I learned with Paul shaped so many decisions I made later on, so many mistakes I now take responsibility for. I don't think I could have ever foreseen where those mistakes would lead me. While 16-year-old me made a bad choice, that crossroads brought me where I am today, despite the painful road it took me on.

Coming from Common Ground

Like all good love affairs, the beginning of my relationship with Paul was passionate in every sense of the word. At the time, all I wanted was to be loved, and Paul showed me the kind of love I was familiar with. It was the kind of passion and pain I'd witnessed between my mother and father. He gave me that feeling of belonging I'd been seeking all my life as well as something else very familiar—the stirrings of chaos. I trusted that it must be "real" love, because there was that tapping I'd grown up with, the tapping that made a house feel like a home. It made me feel like *me* again.

The two of us were quickly inseparable. He knew me better than anyone else in my life at that point, including even Chase and my family. We'd talk for hours, sharing stories of our childhoods and the abuse, fear, and tension that we both understood only too well. Paul had been through enough in his 17 years of life that he made me feel grateful for my own upbringing. We had a lot in common.

Paul was the first person I ever dared to tell about the anxiety I felt. He was the first to know about how my heart would beat frantically in my throat when I'm around too many people. I told him the real reason that I skipped class and why I hated being in public places. He was the first person I had been able to confide in about what I thought made me crazy, the first person with whom I shared my mantra. Rather than seeing me as crazy, he just loved me even more.

Initially I thought I saw in Paul the chance to put my past behind me. He understood the chaos I lived in, and he had hidden his own shame of an abusive family for many years. It seemed to me as if I had found the perfect match, especially since he kept the tapping of chaos alive.

Maybe that is why I remained so in love with him even as the bad times began to outweigh the good. Like my dad, Paul kept me on my toes. I trusted him, but I didn't really feel safe. He fueled the addiction to the chaos I'd learned from my father. I soon realized Paul had his own addictions. All I really knew about drugs was they weren't for me, but I did accept that Paul used pot on a regular basis to cope with his own demons and get him through pretty much everything in life.

I didn't judge Paul's choices. At one point, I actually came to believe that if only I could have hooked up Paul to a steady stream of marijuana, his temper wouldn't have progressively escalated to physical and emotional abuse. He was calmer, more relaxed, and less moody when he smoked—what could be wrong with that? We were both just doing what we had to do to be comfortable in our own skin.

What we didn't realize at the time was that it wasn't our own skin we were trying to be comfortable in. We steadfastly buried the truth of who we were, not even scratching the surfaces of our authentic selves. So of course our temporary fixes and cover-ups were never going to work.

The Power and the Draw of the Tapping

As Paul's marijuana supply became less reliable, his moods got much darker. The chaos in our relationship intensified; but wasn't it my job to make all this work? For the first time in my life, I felt beautiful and fully accepted, something I thought only existed in romantic movies and daydreams. I didn't question the tapping, nor wonder why I instinctively felt fearful of Paul. I was comfortable and I was happy. I started to identify more and more with my mom, and less with that 15-year-old girl who'd been thrown around her kitchen.

I gave up on going to class about two months into the school year and started working night shifts at a coffee shop. Paul quit school at the same time, despite being only months away from receiving his diploma, and replaced classes with parties, alcohol, and marijuana. But who was I to judge? We were teenagers, after all, and madly in love! So with that, Paul and I started our lives together in our own apartment of chaos.

Paul had something about him. He made all the girls feel weak in the knees, and at first it had made me feel so special that out of the entire school, he'd picked *me*. After a while, the self-esteem boost I got when Paul flirted with me faded, and I couldn't quite decide whether this new feeling was my intuition or just my insecurity crawling back. Whatever it was, it only made the tapping grow, and soon I started to understand why.

I remember shivering on the café step after my night shift one January morning. The sun had just risen, and though the temperature was well below freezing, I was hatless and gloveless. (Staying warm was definitely not in fashion at that age.) I was waiting for Paul to pick me up as he usually did, but deep down I knew that he wasn't coming. I'd been feeling for a while as if he were anywhere but with me, not just physically but mentally as well. So I went back inside the café to call the house of a friend where Paul said he would be.

My friend Kayla answered the phone, and I could hear loud music and laughter in the background. She didn't try to hide her disappointment that it was my voice on the other end of the line. She and I had drifted apart since Paul took over my life. She disapproved of my choice to date him and especially to move in with him, as she knew he was completely wrong for me. She didn't know about the draw of the tapping.

"Where's Paul?" I asked. The tapping grew in the pit of my stomach.

"He went to the store with Cathy . . . alone," Kayla said, then fell silent. She didn't really need to say more. It was one of those times I wished I could ignore my intuition and keep on living in blissful ignorance. She'd been right all along, but she cared enough to put aside her anger to tell me the truth. "I'm just saying, there are a bunch of people here, and they're the only two who went to the store. They've been gone over an hour." *Click*—Kayla had hung up.

I still didn't want to believe it. Paul and I were in love! Okay, so we had our problems, but that's no reason to go off with Cathy—why her?

My disbelief slowly turned to anger as I began my long walk home. *I'm leaving him.* I decided this with far less hesitation than I would have expected, given my complete infatuation. I would run away from the tapping and his cheating. I would start again.

My anger had just reached its peak when Paul found me. Every part of my skin that'd been exposed to the frigid air was numb. As he pulled the car alongside me, I yelled at him, pulling out every obscenity that could be expected from a betrayed, heartbroken teenage girl. And he did what every cheating boyfriend does who's been caught: *He denied it.* He told me I had it all wrong, that he'd just gone to the store, and now here he was to come pick me up! He told me over and over how much he loved me, that he wanted to have a family with me. He told me he would never hurt me.

Although I'd been so determined to leave him that I'd already started making plans to find my parents, I hadn't taken into account the power he had over me, even so early in our relationship. Then again, looking back, I really think it was the power of the tapping. Whatever it was, it was too strong for me. I got into the car, and Paul took me home. With every word he spoke, I fell deeper under his spell.

Paul made me feel special in a world that I felt completely crazy in. Slowly I let the anger curl back up in my stomach, into the pit where the anger for my dad also lay. I *wanted* to believe him because I loved him, and I loved being loved. I imagine my mom had similar reasons for staying in her marriage even after the neighbor came by with a shotgun, claiming my dad had been cheating with his wife.

Despite all of Paul's flaws, I knew that deep inside him there was a man who wanted to be good. He struggled with anger issues and addictions most of his life, but he had a conscience. No matter how much he hurt me in the years that followed, I know he loved me. And I think it's because he really loved me that somehow our relationship "worked."

Joy Followed by Loneliness

A few months later, I sat on the side of our small white bathtub, staring at the two blue lines appearing on a little white stick to tell me that I was pregnant. Leaving was no longer an option. The tapping was here to stay.

I smiled from ear to ear with joy. Finally I would have the family I'd always yearned for. Paul was just as ecstatic as I was when I shared the news that I was almost five and a half months pregnant. We didn't have the slightest clue of what it took to raise a family, but between the two of us we certainly had a huge list covered of "what *not* to do." We figured that was good enough!

The next four months weren't quite as exciting. My body changed drastically and so did Paul. He spent more nights partying while I sat at home alone, dreaming of the life I wanted my baby to have. We moved in with one of Paul's friends so we could save money, but I had to quit my job as the new apartment was too far from the coffee shop. I pinched pennies while I looked for another job, but the exhaustion of being pregnant took its toll.

Trying to take my mind off the pain of being home alone all day and night, and fearing the return of my now angry and far-from-passionate boyfriend, I made a trip to the local SPCA. That's when I brought home Bear, a 10-week-old German shepherd mix. He had the cutest little face, and he would never leave my side. He followed me from one room to the next, just excited to be near me. He was the best decision I'd made since meeting Paul—even though I didn't always think so when he made a mess or chewed my favorite shoes!

A few weeks after bringing Bear home, I was woken by his whimpers and cries. My pregnancy had a way of turning me into a zombie at night, so I'm sure it took all of the little puppy's might to rouse me. Bear was pouncing on my face, clawing at me while I struggled to open my eyes. I gave him a playful rub, then got up to check on the faint sound coming from another room. Was it the apartment buzzer? Maybe Paul had forgotten his keys and needed me to let him in.

I was sleepily pressing the talk button on the intercom when I felt an intense heat on my back. With a jolt, I realized that it wasn't the door I was hearing after all—it was the smoke alarm. It buzzed feebly, already half-melted from the flames billowing out of the kitchen. Smoke filled my lungs as I gasped in shock. Snatching Bear tightly to my chest, I ran out the door.

Wailing fire alarms and evacuating tenants greeted me in the hallway. I let Bear's little legs rest on my six-month bump as I made my way outside in a thin cotton nightgown. As soon as my bare feet touched the snowy ground, firefighters whisked me into an ambulance to check me over. I felt numb. Everything I had worked so hard for was gone. The baby clothes I had saved my pennies to buy, the few items I'd managed to pack when I left home at 15—all of it went up in flames as I watched.

Later, the firefighters told me about the butter knives that had been left on our kitchen burner on high heat. That was the source of the fire; Paul had been feeding his escalating drug addiction before work that morning. I didn't even get angry. I embraced the familiar chaos, knowing in that moment we were broke and homeless—and it could only get worse.

A Different Level of Dysfunction

We moved in with Paul's family after the fire. (Unfortunately, we had to find a new home for Bear.) They were dysfunctional in their own way, but they supported me and accepted me into their home with open arms, which was something I desperately needed and am still grateful for. Besides, I was certainly no stranger to dysfunction. There were plenty of family secrets and pain that everyone I knew suffered through, but my 17-year-old self was oblivious to it.

I was nearly seven months pregnant at this point, and Paul still seemed to be struggling with the idea of having a baby on the way. His family, on the other hand, seemed as happy as I was about the coming addition. Their excitement grew along with my belly. Paul started working more and spent a bit more time thinking, drinking, partying, and contemplating (which meant smoking pot).

Looking back, the whole family's addiction to marijuana brought the house a certain mellowness that my own home never had. Paul's father was a recovering alcoholic who attended church and Alcoholics Anonymous meetings religiously. Although he was generally calm, sometimes he'd explode out of nowhere; usually this was when he was out of marijuana. He'd yell and scream, just as my dad did, but his family didn't have the same fear and dread that gripped my family—at least, not that I could see.

I managed to find a job at a government-run afterschool program. It was as much a reason to get out of the house as to help with our bleak financial situation, but shortly after starting I learned how much I *loved* being around kids. Furthermore, even though this was a daytime job surrounded by people, my level of anxiety was utterly manageable!

How excited I was to figure out that I could be around kids without anxiety attacks and crazy thoughts. At the time, I didn't even care why this was, though I now know that it is because young children tend to not have many Spirits around them because they don't yet have many loved ones on the Other Side. I just knew that I could be free and in the moment. It was wonderful to not have to hide who I was out of fear or worry of judgment.

A Date with Destiny

Paul came home from work one day and told me to grab my coat; we were going out to my favorite place, a local Chinese restaurant. It was our idea of a fancy date night, since we didn't have a lot of money. Paul was antsy as we were seated. I could tell there was something on his mind, something itching to get out.

"I'm not scared," he blurted out, sounding as if he were trying to convince himself more than me. He took my hand and stared into my eyes as he continued, "I love you, Carmel. I will stay with you forever, and we will have a beautiful family."

Tears welled in Paul's eyes as he told me that he would never hurt me and never leave me. His face was so full of love, but also pain. He wanted to be different, he wanted to treat me right—at least, I believed so. Surely he just wanted to be loved as much as I did. He seemed to recognize that there was another way, a life different from the abuse we suffered. However, like me, he couldn't seem to figure out *how* to live without that so-familiar chaos.

"Will you marry me?" He slipped a dainty gold band adorned with a humble cluster of diamonds onto my finger.

Of course I said yes! I was smiling ear to ear with excitement and took a moment to admire my new ring. When I looked back up at Paul, the tears were gone and he was concentrating on his food. Apparently, the moment was over. I didn't care, though. I was going to be *married* and have a family!

The charm of Paul's proposal in a threadbare Chinese restaurant was matched by the charm of my pregnancy. I'd been a thin girl—a size eight with some decent curves—but pregnancy changed *that* pretty quickly. There was no "cute" baby bump for others to coo over. Cadbury Caramilk bars had become my new best friends, and it showed. And where was that pregnancy glow I'd heard so much about? I was sweaty, perhaps . . . certainly not glowing.

In a matter of months, Paul had lost his cute and quirky girl-friend, and she'd been replaced with this moodier, 200-pound version. He wasn't really feeling it, and that was the last bit of romance I would see for months to come.

This Guy Is Bad News

Night after night was spent home alone, wondering where Paul was. My self-confidence was in tatters. Then I found a phone number in his pants pocket as I was throwing them in the wash. While part of me had always known he was cheating, another part had been clinging stubbornly to my denial. I'd had a lot of practice, after all.

How could he? I fumed. I was all alone, as usual. *I'm having his baby, and he's off getting numbers?* I could already hear his excuses. "I got it for a friend," he'd say.

But I couldn't take it anymore. I needed to know the truth, and so I confronted him when he came home. Rage boiled up inside me as he finally came clean. "I slept with Cathy," he admitted. The words echoed in my head. Too late to go back now; what's done was done. I wasn't able to hold back my anger for another minute, and we fought longer than we'd ever fought before, right up until he had to leave for work the next afternoon.

I was still crawling the walls when Paul left, so I called Jon, one of the few friends I had left. He was a friend of Paul's older brother, and he had a crush on me that he didn't even attempt to hide. He picked me up and we just sat in his car at the mall. I was yelling and crying at the same time, and I could feel my rage fight against the pain in my heart. I was taken back to that cold January morning, walking alone with no hat or gloves, and my thoughts were exactly the same. I said it out loud, "I'm leaving him."

Jon offered to help. "You've got to get out of there," he told me, as if he'd been biting back those words since he'd met me. "That guy is bad news."

If only I had accepted Jon's advice and his help. I could have gone back to my parents; I could have escaped so much pain if only I'd left that day for good. Instead, I asked Jon to take me back home. I chose the path that was familiar to me. *Tap . . . tap . . . tap . . .*

By the time I was dropped off at home, Paul had already been back for several hours. The fact that I'd been with Jon had already made its way through the rumor mill and back to Paul, who jumped to his own conclusions about what the two of us had been doing. He thought I'd gone looking for revenge rather than escape, and he was boiling with rage.

I had barely set one foot in the house when Paul took hold of my ponytail and yanked me the rest of the way in. Shocked and afraid, I pushed back. "What are you doing?" I screamed.

Paul's eyes were red with anger and they terrified me. All I could think was, *He's gone mad.* He no longer seemed human, but a monster. I'd always been a bit scared of him, just as I'd feared my father, but at the same time I'd never quite believed he could actually physically hurt me. An eerie sense of disbelief settled over me, the same that I felt the day my father beat me. Before he turned and walked away, Paul spit in my face and gave me a look I'd never forget.

Life went back to normal the next day. His apology sounded sincere, and I almost felt comfortable again—at least, until the following Thursday. That's when we fell into a cycle we'd been through numerous times before: "Payday Thursday."

Payday Thursday was the day I'd come to loathe the most. If Paul got paid on a Monday, we'd be okay. When he still had to show up to work for the rest of the week, I had time to buy groceries, pay the bills, and replace some of the baby supplies we'd lost in the fire. But if payday landed on a Thursday, it was a whole different story. I'd wait in vain for Paul to come home from work, hoping that *this* would be the time he'd choose his pregnant fiancée. But deep down, I knew I didn't compare to whatever, or whoever, else it was he did so frequently choose.

Like clockwork, he'd eventually stumble in days later, smelling of booze, sweat, and stale cigarettes. He had everyone else to blame and a million stories. Each time was a little bit worse, and each time I forgave him.

I justified it to myself in my head. It was my job to keep my family together, after all. Fatherhood would change him, we'd soon see—our first daughter was on her way.

Growing Our Family

Melissa was born a healthy 7 pounds and 14 ounces, after three whole days of labor. Three days of pain and agony and swearing that I'd never do it again. But the moment I saw her beautiful eyes for the first time, all the pain melted away. She stole our hearts. Not just mine and Paul's hearts, either—Paul's whole family was head over heels in love with her, and she became their princess. *Our* little princess, and *my* new family.

In a stunning coincidence, Melissa wasn't the only one who joined my and Paul's family that day. Only hours after Melissa entered this world, my *old* family reappeared, too. Likely it was my mom's intuition, strong as always, that led her to contact me at that moment. She tracked down the phone number of Paul's family home, and Paul's brother answered her call. "She's not here right now. She's in the hospital having a baby," he told her bluntly.

I nearly fell over in fear when the nurse came into my room to say that my father was on the phone for me. I was changing (or attempting to change) Melissa, and I had to put her down as my whole body went weak. *How did he find me?* I was overwhelmed by the same fear I felt the last time I'd seen my family, as a 15-year-old girl escaping his tyranny. Shaking, I took the phone—I was scared, tired, and still really angry.

But instead of the ranting I expected, I heard love and pride in my father's voice. "I'm so sorry, Carmel. We love you so much, and we are so happy for you," he said. He burst out crying, and I could feel his emotions hit me. My father was over the moon to be a biological grandfather for the first time. Melissa, his first granddaughter . . . it was me, all over again. *The champagne, the pedestal, all of it,* I thought, *it's hers.*

"What do you need? You could have called us! We can send money, or a plane ticket, just let us know. We are here for you," he said it all with such sincerity. I could scarcely believe it.

True to their word, my parents sent me a plane ticket to see them in BC once Melissa was old enough to fly. So, for the first time in years, I went back home. It was something I'd sworn never to do, but I needed their help more than ever.

I recognized very little in their new place, at least very few physical items. Although we'd learned never to become attached to any object, I still looked for one item in particular: my nana's gold and red tin box. I was devastated to learn that they no longer had it, but there was nothing I could do.

As Melissa and I settled in, I felt the old familiar tension, which had always been the one constant in their home and in my life. Perhaps that's why I felt so comfortable when I arrived. The chaos and tapping were still there—it even seemed to have increased in strength. The chaos in my own life had intensified as well, but for once I was grateful for my parents' ability to cover the truth and pretend everything was just fine. I had my own shit to deal with, after all; I didn't have time for theirs. I was just happy to have them back in my life, false appearances and all.

By now I had also gotten very good at covering up my truth with lies of shame. I wasn't about to tell my parents about the tension in my own home. I didn't mention Paul's temper or his drug problems. Even when I received a phone call from Paul's family with news of his latest betrayal, I just kept smiling, dying a little more inside with each passing day.

When I left my parents' house, I knew very well that I was walking back into chaos. But I was determined to hold firm in my power on my return. I may have been denying Paul's cheating to everyone else, but I was not going to deny it in my own home any longer. This time I would confront him; I would stand strong. I wasn't putting up with any more of his crap.

I had a clear picture of the life I wanted for myself and my daughter as we returned home. But life did not unfold the way I saw it in my head.

.

Chapter Six

TILL DEATH DO US PART

As luck would have it, I came back to an empty home; it was Payday Thursday. Paul didn't come home that night, as usual. But unlike so many Thursdays in the past, this time I didn't stay up waiting for him. I was relieved to have a bit of a break from Paul, from our fighting, but I knew deep down that the timing couldn't have been worse.

I smelled fermented beer and stale cigarettes, and felt his rage even before I saw his face. He'd come home hungover—and ready to fight. As the yelling between us grew louder, Melissa woke up crying. I continued to tell Paul what an asshole he was, speaking in an angry whisper, as I soothed Melissa in her crib. I hoped she would drift back into her dreams, oblivious to the pain building up around her. But Paul didn't get the hint, as usual, and continued to yell.

I knew that the tension from the house was now seeping into my baby's tiny body. I hated knowing that she was being roped into the same chaos I myself had become addicted to. As Melissa lay there quiet and comfortable amid the explosive situation, I couldn't take it anymore. I was not going to be my mother. There would be no false appearances in my home, no more chaos tapping on my newborn girl's perfect, milky-white skin. I couldn't make this work. I didn't want to make this work.

"We are done. I'm leaving."

Running for Dear Life

That's when Paul hit me. The back of his hand came down across my face so hard that I was surprised not to find myself on the floor. I didn't hesitate a moment; I immediately grabbed Melissa's diaper bag and reached for her. But as I moved passed Paul toward the crib, he yanked at my hair so hard that I screamed. I immediately threw my hand over my mouth to avoid frightening Melissa as Paul dragged me out of the room by my hair and spat at me: "You're not taking her anywhere." I didn't doubt the threat I heard in his voice, and fear surged within me as I looked him straight in his bloodshot eyes.

I didn't want to leave Melissa, but it was now or never. I bolted for the front door. I kicked his grasping hands away as he tried to pull me down the stairs. I flew out the door and ran for help, for my life and my daughter's. I was in a full sprint toward the payphone across the street when I heard Paul screaming my name.

I didn't want to stop. Paul was faster than me, and if I paused to see what he wanted, I would lose the slim advantage of my head start. I tried to move, but I felt paralyzed, though only for a second.

"Turn around." It was a man's voice, clear as day, but it wasn't Paul. It felt as if someone had come up beside me and spoke into my ear, stern but not angry. The voice grew more urgent: "Turn around, right now!"

Startled and panicked, I turned around. The terror I saw then would control me for years to come. In that moment, I knew Paul had won, and I would never get away. The tension wasn't my dad's anymore; it was Paul's and he was worse. Paul's eyes were full of an intense determination as he dangled Melissa by her feet, as if she were a ragdoll to be discarded into the snow.

I opened my mouth, but nothing came out. I was still paralyzed, confused by the voices I heard and terrified by the sight of my daughter in danger. Paul screamed, "You better get back here right now, or I'm going to drop her in this fucking snow bank, I swear to God. Don't think I won't!"

Before he could finish his last words, my feet were moving again, racing back to save my daughter. I was so relieved to have Melissa in my arms again, but in that moment, my life changed forever. It went from salvageable to hopeless. From near freedom to firmly entrapped. Paul's hand wrapped around my neck as he hissed, "If you ever leave, I will kill her and then I will kill you." He spat in my face again and pushed me toward our front door.

From that point on, Paul controlled my every movement. I curled my body around my daughter, struggling to protect her from the monster her father had become. I'd barely laid her in her crib before I was ripped out of her room once more. This time, I was down on the floor throughout my beating. I felt every kick and hit, but I also felt numb. Why would I be surprised? This was my life, my chaos. It's what I knew. It's what I chose.

I deserve this, I almost convinced myself. *This is what men do.*

Navigating the Cycle of Pain and Love

I spent the next few nights planning and plotting, trying to figure out how to run away without putting Melissa's life in danger; deep inside, I knew it was too late. Meanwhile, Paul snapped out of being a monster and transitioned into what I now call "suck-up mode." Every minute was spent convincing me that he loved me. He pined and promised never to hurt me again. He kissed me and loved me with a passion I hadn't seen since the days we were first together. Before long I was lulled by the familiar sense of belonging, back in the cycle of what I believed to be true love.

From that point on, our relationships was a roller coaster of pain and love. There'd be big blowouts, after which he'd apologize, and I'd always forgive him. Perhaps he needed to see the physical marks he made on my body to realize he'd gone too far; that seemed to be his trigger back to "old" Paul. He'd stop going to the bar, and would be all about me—gentle, kind, loving, passionate. But of course, the monster would slowly creep back in. Soon I learned to live with it, caught in a familiar cycle with no way out.

In the 13 years I was with Paul, I never once called the police on him. I was so ashamed and felt so stupid that I allowed my husband to do this to me and my children. I knew in my heart this was wrong, but I also knew that I loved him. One day, I believed, he would change.

Even though I swore I wouldn't, I became a master of false appearances, just like my mother. Our home always looked great despite our inability to pay the bills. We got good at moving on a day's notice, sometimes forced out of our home when we couldn't gather enough cash to pay and the landlord wouldn't give us any more breaks. But I set some ground rules: never a new school, never new friends. My kids would not face continuously starting again with nothing, the way I had. As a result, our life became a game of musical chairs around the same neighborhood.

Another Child, Another Reprieve

I soon learned a trick or two about keeping Paul under control. Shortly after finding out I was pregnant for the second time, I noticed that while Paul would be emotionally abusive—calling me a useless whore, cheating on me, pushing me around a bit—he wouldn't physically beat me if I was carrying a child. Soon those round cheeks and growing thighs I had despised so much in my first pregnancy became my protection against Paul's ever more frequent explosions. It was my only defense and I used it over the years, getting pregnant as quickly as I could after giving birth. It's probably not often that women think of pregnancy as saving their body from pain, but for me that's what it did. It saved me, and it brought me four beautiful children.

I went into labor with my second child shortly after our fourth move. This time was much quicker than the first, with no drugs necessary. Within six hours, we had a healthy, 9 pounds and 1 ounce, bouncing baby boy. Paul couldn't have been happier, as he was the third in a line of Pauls and wanted to extend the tradition.

Only minutes after his son was born, Paul left to celebrate. He flew out of the room, telling me that he'd be back after a quick celebratory drink. When he returned, shaking me awake at 3 A.M., I could tell by the stench that he didn't stop after just one. He pushed me out of bed. I had just given birth, but *he* needed to rest, apparently. I was forced to curl up in the small armchair in the corner while he crawled into my bed and fell asleep.

When the nurse came into the room and saw me stiff and curled up in the armchair, she called security, kicking Paul out of the hospital for the duration of my stay. "You need to leave him," she told me. She gave me the same look of pity and sympathy I'd seen so many times; that look I always chose to ignore.

Although I knew the nurse was right—they all were—something in me wouldn't admit it to myself. As hurt and upset as I was by everything Paul had done to me, I still loved him just as much as I did when we first fell in love. By now, I'd accepted Paul's actions and my own choices in my life. But as I held my new baby boy in my arms, my heart ached. I thought of how my actions would one day impact him, too.

The doctor came in my room the next morning and cheerfully said, "We need to give this little guy a name." Paul and I had never had a conversation about naming our second child, probably because neither of us ever thought it needed to be discussed. Any boy, of course, would become the fourth to carry on the family name. The fourth man in a line of alcoholics and addicts. I looked into this angel's eyes and felt sorry for him. Something just didn't sit right with me about that name.

When I was quite young, my grandma had told me that the names we are given in life mean something. Each name, she said, holds with it a sort of energy, and attached to it is your life's purpose. Despite my love for Paul, I couldn't force myself to pass on that name, that energy, and that life path to my innocent little boy.

The nurse watched me fill out the form, and I caught her smile as she saw what I had done. Instead of Paul's family name, I gave my son my own family name. I gave him the first name of Wayne, after my father, and the middle name of Kevin, after my brother. Perhaps you might still think of my father as a monster, too, but by now I had come to see him in a different light. After all, he was the first man to love and care for me.

I felt so powerful, like I was freeing my son from the tyranny of a legacy he shouldn't be saddled with. *Wayne,* I thought fondly. In the box for the father's name, I wrote what I'd been hoping for in that moment: *Unknown.*

Where There's Smoke, There's Fire

Once at home, I clung to Wayne the same way I had clung to the safety of my pregnancy. I was scared to put him down. I knew that my safety net had been whisked away, and I was worried that Paul would return to his old ways any day now. Which, of course, he did. The chaos of our lives fell into a consistent routine: the ever-present tapping would get stronger, Paul would blow up at me violently, then there would be a quiet honeymoon period where he was so, so sorry. On it went, over and over and over again.

Yes, I threatened to leave. Sometimes I did leave, with the children in tow. And every time, Paul would beg me to come back, pledging to go to Alcoholics Anonymous, to quit drinking, to quit drugs, to commit to his family. He'd make big promises, but he had no reason to follow through. After all, I always accepted his words at face value and went back to him.

We had just moved into a townhouse not far from our previous apartment when I found out I was pregnant with our third child. The timing was perfect because I could feel the tapping getting stronger. Paul was deep into his alcoholism and headed for a blowup, but my new baby bump meant a new safety blanket. However, while the beatings stopped, Paul acquired an arrogance that told me that there was someone else. He no longer cared what I knew and what I didn't. I was finding not only phone numbers, but love notes in his pockets.

I might have thought I was worthless when Paul and I first met, broken by what my dad had done to me, but looking back now I see that day was only the beginning. Now I also felt powerless against Paul's threats. I didn't just have myself and Melissa to protect anymore, I had Wayne and soon I'd have our third child, a little girl we'd name Jessica. I could justify why I stayed all I want, but the truth was that I didn't know *how* to leave. This was the only kind of life I had ever really known.

One morning, I was awakened by the thick and horrible taste of smoke. Although I'd become used to sleeping alone in bed, I panicked not knowing where Paul was. I recognized this—*another fire*. The fire alarm was blaring, and the smoke had grown so thick I couldn't see down the stairs to know where it was coming from or what was going on. I began screaming for Paul, and he suddenly appeared bewildered and shocked at the bottom of the stairs. "Stay there! I got this!" he yelled.

I ran back to our bedroom and opened the window to get air; I didn't realize what a mistake that would be! It caused smoke to billow through my room, and I gasped at the screen for air. I knew I had to get out. I quickly grabbed little Jessica, only a couple months old, and held my breath as I made my way down the stairs and out the door. Paul ran past me on his way up the stairs, yelling that he would get Melissa and Wayne. I could smell the whiskey on him and see him struggling for balance against his booze-induced haze, but Paul successfully retrieved both Wayne and Melissa.

Then, to my horror, the firefighters revealed that the fire was started by a pot of French fries that Paul must have begun cooking in a drunken stupor before passing out on the couch. It dawned on me the true harm that this man was putting our family in, and I vowed that I was going to leave him. How could I be with this man? He was completely out of his mind! I told myself that it was over; I was really leaving this time.

Facing My Own Reality

My new resolve lasted 24 hours. Again, Paul claimed he was going to change, and again I believed him.

Although we'd moved too many times to count by now, the devastation of the fire prompted my parents to travel to help us with the move this time. They offered to help us recover some of our lost belongings, since they knew we couldn't afford to do it on our own, but there also seemed to be a little extra motivation to visit. My father was pushing for us to get married, and he suggested that we do so while he and my mother were visiting.

Maybe my dad thought that the vows would make Paul shape up and begin taking his role as a husband and father more seriously. My dad didn't know (at least, I don't think he knew) that Paul was physically abusive. At the same time, money was equal to love for my dad, so in his eyes, Paul wasn't doing nearly enough to provide properly for me and the children. Nonetheless, my father kept pushing for months for a wedding.

The story of our wedding is a short one. We booked Pastor Ken and rented a hall for the reception. We told our friends and family. Paul celebrated the night before by getting himself put in jail for drunk driving and was hit with a DUI charge, which I should have taken as a clue as to where my marriage might be heading. But, no I didn't see it. Instead, my brother bailed him out, and the next day we were holding hands in church, me in a crisp white dress.

Paul put a small gold wedding band on my ring finger and smiled, his eyes rising to connect with mine. I became lost in my own thoughts as I stood there in front of our friends and family. I thought back through all of the decisions I had made that landed me there on that day, declaring my love to this man: the first man to capture my heart, the first of so many things, but the second man to teach me to need the chaos, to crave the tapping. I thought back to the day that I chose Paul over Chase. I could remember that day in school as if it were yesterday, but in truth it was five years ago . . . and so much had changed since.

It was our wedding, and I was still in love with Paul then; but what did *I* know about love? I was marrying the man who stole my heart, but also my voice. He controlled me emotionally and physically. "For better or for worse," echoed in my head, and I pushed away all my memories of the latter. I caught the disappointment in my mother's glance as I snapped back into the present to say: "I do."

Maybe my mother was disappointed because she could tell I was not really present. But, more likely, she had recognized that look on my face. After all, it was a look she'd worn herself most of her life. It was an expression of denial, denying the pain and the cheating, convincing yourself it was in your head; believing that the *better* somehow justified the *worse*. As the small crowd clapped and shouted out to congratulate us, I had to look away from my mother. She was the one person who could see right through me.

Wearing the mask of denial is not something we do consciously. I think we do it instinctively to protect ourselves and to protect those we love. We can smile and laugh while denying our truth, without even knowing we are doing it. Whatever our truth—our sexuality, our past or present belief systems, or what we put up with in our intimate relationships—somehow it often seems easier to hide than to accept it.

Watching Paul dance in his crisp tux with four-year-old Melissa standing adorably on his shoes, I smiled and placed my hand on my stomach. I knew something no one else did; I was pregnant again. My fourth child, Emily, was on the way. Some people may never understand how I managed to love this man, but he (and the tapping) was all I knew.

Truth be told, without Paul, I wouldn't be who I am today. As you know, I have come to believe in my heart that we pick the people we trust the most on the Other Side to teach us the toughest life lessons on this side. Something deep down within me knew that my love for Paul was the answer to finding my life's purpose.

Even if it nearly killed me, those 13 difficult years with him were what ultimately helped me find my authentic self, become a healer, and later change the lives of so many others. Unfortunately, I still had a few more stiff lessons to learn before I could truly step into my own authentic life . . . along with a battle to fight that threatened everything I tried so hard to keep safe.

Chapter Seven

PANIC 101

Today was the day; my life was going to get back on track. I was going to get myself and my kids out of the marriage that was slowly breaking me beyond repair. Some days, it took all I could do just to hold things together. With our family growing and my parents living far away, I was depending more and more on Paul's family to help us out. Melissa was five years old now, and Paul's parents would take her on outings and often let her stay at their house—a shelter for her from the chaos growing inside our little duplex in Mill Woods, a suburb of Edmonton. It was a great help to me, but I was worried about the special treatment she received. I recognized the patterns in Melissa's childhood, so similar to my own, that led to my addiction to the tapping.

Paul's drinking had gotten out of control at this point, and I was pretty sure there was more than alcohol circulating his blood stream. With him often coming home incoherent and out of his mind, I had to use all my wits to keep us safe; my intuition kept us just one step ahead of danger.

One of the things I was particularly worried about was another fire. So whenever Paul was out drinking heavily, I'd turn off the electrical breaker to the stove. That way, if he decided to put something on to cook, the stove wouldn't work! It made him furious when he'd come rolling in drunk as a lord and hungry, but eventually he figured out to reset the breaker. When I realized he'd caught on to me, I started pulling the stove out from the wall, unplugging it from the electrical socket, then sliding it back into place. Paul never figured out *that* particular trick, and I was able to rest in bed at night more peacefully. I still chuckle each time I think back to those times. As dark a game as it was, it kept us safe from another fire, so the effort was well worth it.

With Paul's drinking and drug use back in full force, I began to worry: *What if Melissa was learning to crave the tapping?* My heart ached to think of her ending up like me, like my mother, stuck in the cycle of chaos. So I did the only thing I could think of to change the outcome—I was going back to high school to try again.

Pushing the Panic Button

I parked my car and walked into my new school with confidence. Things were looking up for me! Paul's parents bought me driving lessons for my 24th birthday, and my dad had helped me get a car just a few weeks ago. It was a used car, but it was the first one I'd ever owned. I'd so badly wanted a car ever since my brother Kevin had gotten one when we moved away from Leduc. It had been his escape from the chaos, allowing him to come and go as he pleased. I thought that it would be my ticket to freedom, too. I thought I was taking the first step toward getting my children a better life than I had. Unfortunately for me, it turned into a different story.

When I reached the building, I walked right into an elevator full of people without thinking twice. Now *that* turned out to be a mistake! A metal box, full of people—I realized a second too late that this was not going to end well.

Before I knew it, the doors closed, trapping me in a small room with all those people. At the same time I felt a metal vice close in around my chest, squeezing out all of my air, throwing me into a sudden state of fear. That newfound confidence was gone; all I could think about was dying. The whole building felt as if it was falling down around me. What I'd felt before in Mr. Thompson's class, and the anxiety attacks I'd struggled with ever since, didn't even compare to this wave of panic. This truly felt like *death* looming over me, seeping inside me, and taking over my entire body.

My old mantra of "I'm crazy" took a step back that day. While being overwhelmed by fear and anxiety, I didn't just think that I was crazy; I was *sure* I was dying. Although I'd felt anxiety before, I'd always been able to move or walk away, and as soon as I left the crowded place, the sensation would immediately stop. But this was the end—I knew it. This time, it was *not* stopping.

My heart pounded in my chest. I became dizzy, and I just couldn't catch my breath. I was swirling around like I was losing my mind. My chest hurt like hell and my heart was going 100 miles a minute. My lips were numb, and I gasped for air. When the elevator doors finally opened again, I flew out of there.

If only I had known then, what I know now. Now I know that when Spirits want to communicate, they come in close around me and affect the energy around my physical body. It causes me to feel all kinds of things emotionally, physically, and mentally. To this day, each and every reading I give begins with similar sensations; it feels to me almost like a pre-anxiety attack. I feel like I'm a plane about to take off, but now that I know the truth of what's happening, I can stay in control and drive the plane where I need it to go.

But I didn't know any of this while I was experiencing my first full-blown panic attack. If I hadn't been trapped in fear and denial, if I could have accepted my truth, maybe things would have gone differently. Looking back now, it wasn't just the first of an increasing number of panic attacks; this was the first day of a life of seclusion and fear, the day I gave up on a *dream*.

Starting Over and Desperate for Answers

The intense fear that flooded my body in that elevator stopped me from entering the classroom I wanted so badly to be in. It stomped on my hopes and dreams. I mustered every ounce of strength in my body to fight against the pain, the fear, and the helplessness, but all the strength in the world could not make my legs move. Nothing could get me into that classroom. Instead, I was waiting for my heart to calm down and hiding in the cafeteria—*again.*

The worst part of all this was that I'd pushed so hard to convince everyone I could do it. I'd had to convince Paul, myself . . . even the government! I'd needed to get a student loan, since at my age, I had to pay for the courses. And now I was back to where I began. I was back in the cafeteria. *Great,* I thought to myself. *Now what?*

I sipped some apple juice and sighed with relief as the panic attack slowly faded away. Still, I knew that consequences faced me at home once Paul learned of my failure. Filled with defeat, I walked back to my car, only to find chaos waiting for me right inside. I slipped into another panic attack, just as strong as the one I felt in the elevator. Another took over me the next day when I went to the grocery store. Each time I was sure I was dying, and each time I felt more and more defeated.

Panic became my constant companion, and my life got smaller and smaller. I drove my car, once a promising symbol of freedom, only a handful of times after that first panic attack. Like the elevator in the school, my car turned into one of the many triggers that started the panic attacks. So I stopped driving. As the car sat idle, Paul had one more reason to be mad at me, as if he needed any reason at all.

Although driving was no longer an option, neither was the bus. Any time I left the house, my heart would begin to explode. The triggers were everywhere: the grocery store, the bank, the sidewalk, the park. Once that door was open, I could no longer avoid the triggers the way I did before. Something was medically wrong with me now, I was sure, but I had no idea what.

The severity of my panic attacks continually landed me in a building with the worst triggers of all: *the hospital.* Throughout my life, I'd always avoided hospitals as much as I could. I knew that the feelings and crazy voices were worse there for some reason. Now I know that it's the large number of scared, dying, and newly dead people in hospitals that make them so difficult for me to be in. At the time, I just saw it as one of so many places that caused me to lose control of my own thoughts.

After that first panic attack, Paul and I spent hour after hour in emergency rooms at least once or twice a month. Doctor after doctor would look at me like I was crazy, and Paul seemed like he was starting to believe them, too. After seeing on the monitor how fast my heart was racing, doctors would say, "That's impossible . . . how are you even standing?" I felt like saying to them, "Why don't you tell me? You're the doctor!"

They would test my blood, my lungs, and my brain, then send me home with mobile heart-rate monitors; but nothing ever came of the tests and readings. According to them, *nothing* was wrong with me, nothing physical, at least. You're *just* having a panic attack, they'd say. It's all in your head, I was told. They suggested that it was caused by my smoking, so I quit; nothing changed. The symptoms remained.

The doctors used words I had never heard of before, so I looked them up. What did a diagnosis of panic and anxiety as a medical condition mean? I didn't *just* feel anxious; I felt like I was going to *die*. No, I *knew* I was going to die. Was that what they meant by *anxiety* or was that *panic*? Or neither? The more I looked into these new diagnoses, the more the pieces started to fit together in my life. *Okay, so this is what's wrong with me,* I thought.

But this answer didn't make me feel better. If anything, it made me feel worse. Now I had one more thing to be ashamed of, and one more thing to hide. My only hope of avoiding the shame was in the doctors' hands, or so I thought. Once the doctors had managed to label my problem, the next step was to figure out the root cause and how to treat it. I believed a solution must be right around the corner. Wasn't that how medicine worked? The hard part, as I understood it, was the diagnosis; after that was settled, the cure should be straightforward.

Searching for Solutions

The first drug the doctors put me on made me so dizzy and nauseated I didn't even last the minimum recommendation of three weeks. I remember trying to help my sister Tracy at work one day while I was on this medication. She had moved back to Edmonton by this time and owned a restaurant in nearby Fort Saskatchewan. Even with my best efforts, I soon found myself huddled on the floor at the back in the kitchen, desperately holding on to my head to try to get it to stop spinning. This was *not* the cure I was looking for!

The second drug they put me on was no better. I'd lose control of my thoughts, my heart, *and* my breathing. So not only was I dying now, but I was also back to being crazy. I threw the bottle of pills in the garbage where it met the other failed bottle. Drugs, I decided, just weren't for me.

But now what? If they knew *what* was wrong with me, why didn't they know how to fix it? The doctors told me I just needed to keep trying different drugs, that one would work for me eventually, but I felt too scared, too weak, and too broken. I waved my white flag and retreated back to my little world, which had become limited to the confines of my bedroom. Although I shared this space with my monster husband, he was no longer the source of my worst fears; I was more frightened of what was *inside* me.

By this time, so stressed out by the panic and anxiety, I started to feel more anger for Paul than love. I still cared for him deeply, but how long could I continue to drown in all this emotional pain? I'd lay awake on the couch and think back to the nurse who told me I should have left Paul when Wayne was born. I'd think of Chase, of my mom, of Kayla—I knew they had all been right. They saw the chaos as danger, and they warned me, even begged me, to get away.

The emotional bruises began to hurt me more than any of the physical bruises ever did. I found myself wishing Paul would hit me again, because it was better than the pain he could inflict with just the words from his mouth. I felt like the most awful person in the world; I deserved nothing and no one. I felt like everything I did was wrong. I could feel myself becoming harder, angrier, and vindictive. Still, here I was, locking myself in a room with this awful man because I was even more scared of the panic that awaited me outside the walls of our house.

This was the beginning of my unraveling. I could feel myself losing that last little spark of who I was, and I knew I had to get out once and for all. I was becoming *him*.

A Whole New World?

Taking a page from my mother's book, I packed up the kids, told them we were going on holiday to Grandma's, and put us all on a bus to Vancouver Island, British Columbia. As we got closer, I called up my older brother Trevor to tell him that Paul was an emotionally abusive cheater. It didn't matter that my family wasn't always around, each of them had a way of stepping up when I needed them most.

Opening up to my family gave me the courage to stick to my guns. It helped that Paul had gotten to know Trevor well, and so knew enough to fear him. I would never tell my brother that Paul hit me, because I worried about what he would do. So I just played it down and told him that I refused to live in the same house as Paul anymore. My brother paid to move all of our stuff back to BC, and before I knew it we were back to where my own life began. This time we didn't have the peach trees, the pools, and the money. But I felt safer and started trying to rebuild my life.

My mother and I were now in the same small town as each other, living similar lives. She'd finally found the courage to leave her marriage, so my father was no longer living with her. We were both learning to be *ourselves*, without the men who had defined us for so long. We were both learning to live without the chaos and the tapping. It was a whole new world. Slowly, we built up our lives and our relationship together.

We had both escaped, but neither of us realized just how different it would feel now that the tapping was gone. It was an uncomfortable sensation. You just don't know how to live without the pain you've had for so long. I don't know about my mother, but as for myself, I felt like my skin wasn't my own anymore. I still craved the chaos without knowing consciously what was wrong.

It's a hard and complicated thing to put into words. Those who have endured abuse may have had this same feeling. You may even understand why I answered when Paul called, and why I let him in under my skin again. Because sure enough, Paul spent the next three months cleaning up his act. He went to Alcoholics Anonymous, he went to work, and he called me every day to tell me he was sorry. I let myself get pulled back into the chaos one conversation at a time because it was what made me feel more comfortable, more like myself.

When I was away from Paul I had to explain to others why we broke up. I had to face the past I had chosen, somehow explain my addiction to the chaos. It was not an easy thing to talk about. But when I was back with my husband, I was *normal*.

So, three months later, Paul moved to BC to be with me.

An Answer for Everything

In my mind, living with Paul was somehow better than living alone because the shame was easier to hide. Either way, I had to cope with the panic that had taken over my life, but being alone added another level of shame because I was also a single mother. I felt that if I raised the kids by myself and did it all wrong, then I would be the only one to blame. It was easier for me to blame Paul for everything than to stand up and be accountable myself. As you can see, I was now a master at justifying everything.

At first, Paul got a job at a mill that my uncle referred him to, but the pay wasn't nearly as much as the union job he had in Alberta. It definitely wasn't enough to afford the house and all the bills. I thought about trying to work as well, but I couldn't drive or be in public because of my panic attacks.

I was so full of shame that I would lie about why I couldn't go out, and why I didn't play a greater role in my kids' lives. I lied about why I couldn't attend parent–teacher interviews or go shopping when the stores were full. I hadn't even realized I had developed so much shame, but the lies just kept getting more and more detailed. I had an answer for everything.

As my lies grew, so did Paul's. Paul and my brother Trevor formed a working relationship that very quickly started to worry me, because neither of them kept me in the loop about what was going on. The bond between them grew stronger until suddenly I wasn't the closest one to my brother anymore. Paul seemed to be gone a lot, doing steroids with my brother, and taking on my brother's beliefs and codes about life.

At this point Paul wasn't beating me, but I suspected that he was back to cheating on me. Even worse, I suspected that my brother knew. You have to understand Trevor's morals: he believed that you make love with your wife, but you have sex with other women. My father hadn't raised his sons to respect women; we'd learned from him that cheating was perfectly acceptable in a man's world. Paul now had his freedom and an ally to protect him, and all I had was a world that was getting smaller and smaller and smaller.

No Way Out of a Very Small World

Due to my panic and anxiety, I was hardly leaving the house now. I remember wanting to check the mail one morning, but I didn't think I could walk across the street to the mailbox. I felt paralyzed. I had given the fight a fair effort, but I knew now that panic was winning. I fell deeper into depression, suffering daily with anxiety, fear, and anger, and all of it was tethered to my shame.

I hated who I had become, but I didn't want anyone else to know. I was trapped in my own world and lost sight of everything else happening around me. The world kept moving, but I stood still. When my mom found out that her father was very sick with cancer, I was no help, even though I felt terrible that I couldn't support her when she needed me most. My mom continued to worry about me, all the while trying to take care of him. I don't know how she did it.

When my aunt and uncle saw the added stress I was putting on my mother, they decided to bring me a computer one day. They hoped it would help push me out of my shell and bring me back to life. They said there was this new thing called the *Internet* (hard to believe there was a time we didn't have it!) and people could use it to research things from all over the world. It was perfect, they thought, to help me remember what was happening outside of my small world, and perhaps inspire me to get out and involve myself more in my children's lives.

Their intentions were good, but their gift ended up doing just the opposite for me. My mom struggled in her grief after her father died, while I just dug myself deeper into my own online world, spending endless hours each day in chat rooms and playing games. Rather than wanting to leave my four-walled cage, I was becoming more and more comfortable in this new Internet world. It was an amazing place where I could be someone else entirely, someone I preferred so much more than the "real life" me who was crazy and so screwed up.

Paul hated the computer. He would go to work and come home, and I'd still be in the same place he left me. He wanted dinner on the table and the house clean, but I was too busy creating a new and improved "online me" to even care about his needs or even the children's. I did only the bare minimum. I would come out of my room to make dinner or do a load of laundry, just enough to barely get by, but I was in total survival mode.

My mother watched helplessly as I withdrew even further into my own world, hiding from the world outside, the one with my children in it. She didn't understand why I chose the computer over my family. Some days she became so frustrated with me, she'd physically pull me out of my room. She'd look at me with those disappointed eyes I remembered from my teen years. "You've just *got* to plug back into your family, Carmel!" she'd beg me.

I knew she was really desperate when she enlisted Paul to help. He would have been the last person she'd have ever wanted to spend an afternoon with. "We are going out for the afternoon, Carmel, and you're coming. No questions asked," she said firmly. She might as well have told me she was taking me to be executed.

Out? I thought. *I can't go out. Outside with people? Outside with the panic? Outside where I can't hide who I am and that I am crazy?*

The moment I entered the pub that my mother and Paul had dragged me out to, I knew I'd made a mistake. "I forgot my sweater," I gasped—or some other, equally lame excuse—and escaped to the car. I collapsed to the floor, clutching at my chest, willing my exploding heart to calm down. I was shaking, clenching my teeth, crying, and begging to be back in the comfort of my room, away from the people and the panic that was taking over my life. I prayed to God to help me, to make me normal, to make my mom the queen, to make all the lies I ever told true.

When my mother found me curled up and trembling in the car, she didn't say a word. Her silence was enough to tell me how scared she was for me. They had no choice but to take me home. I doubt that my mother knew what a disaster it would be to drag me out of my room that day, but now she understood how seriously I was affected. She called a counselor and made me an appointment that same day. When I didn't go to the appointment, she brought the counselor to me.

Rejoining the World Already in Progress

Although the strategy of speaking to a counselor was good, unfortunately the advice was the same: drugs. "No, thank you," I said to the doctor, thinking back to my failed experience with the two that I'd already tried. But my new doctor insisted that this drug was different. "It will stop an anxiety attack right in its tracks." That certainly was different, considering the other drugs only managed to cause me more anxiety. There was no three-week trial, no adjustment period, just results. The sales pitch worked. He certainly was a good drug dealer, a legal one at that.

Soon I was an Ativan believer. Right away, that pill became my air supply. It wasn't exactly a miracle drug, but it did manage to get me out of my room. Before, I'd been completely unplugged from the world outside of the computer, and my kids had been the ones who paid the price. Once I had Ativan as my backup, I was able to spend a little more time outside of my room. I became a bit more engaged with the kids and their lives. I was able to drive them to their sports games and sometimes even pick them up from school, though I still couldn't get out of the car.

This tiny pill under my tongue meant that fear no longer controlled my whole life, but the anxiety didn't completely disappear. I don't think there were enough small white pills to ever get me into that school, among so many parents and cheering fans. I always had an excuse anyway. I needed to get groceries, maybe, or clean the house. Grocery shopping was a bad excuse—the kids knew I never did that—but it sounded plausible to most people. Stores were still one of the places I hadn't been able to go since the first panic attacks, and it remained so even with the new pills.

I had somewhat of a life back, but no pill could get rid of the shame I had built that life on top of. I was much more comfortable with the life I had created online. I could talk with whoever wanted to talk back, and I turned it into a game to figure out who was lying, who was hiding shame like me, and who was trustworthy. Being on a computer didn't trigger my panic or anxiety, and my intuition still seemed to be spot on. I never even thought twice about the intuitive thoughts I had about each person—the red flags, or the lack thereof. I just considered myself a great judge of people. I thought I just always had that natural talent, like my mother.

I reinvented myself online and gave this persona a new name: *Heather*. She was who I wanted to be: strong, no nonsense, confident, funny. Heather had no shame and nothing to hide. I loved being her. It was too bad "Heather" couldn't take my kids to school. For that, I had to be Carmel, and I had to rely on the pills. And as Carmel, living in the real world, I had to deal with the good and the bad that Ativan brought me.

Little did I know that I would soon be dealing with the good and the bad that Heather would be bringing to me. Believe me, all that turned into quite the adventure! My life would soon be taking a few unexpected turns on my way to discovering my authentic self. I'd even be doing some globetrotting.

Maybe I could find true love after all—not only for the man I was supposed to be with, but also for myself? I really hoped so.

Chapter Eight

SHADES OF GRAY

Ativan drew all of the colors out of my life, leaving everything in a pale shade of gray. But this was a small price to pay for fitting in. Soon I was as attached to those pills as I was to cigarettes and a lighter when I still smoked. Before leaving the house, Ativan was the first thing I checked for. *Ativan, check; keys, check; purse, check— okay, I'm good to go.*

This little pill was the one thing that could stop me from going crazy and helped me claw my way back to normalcy. Or at least to what I thought *normal* was. I had spent so much of my life trying to be what I thought everyone else wanted me to be, and I thought this pill would finally allow me to do that. The side effect, though, was that I no longer saw color. I don't mean this literally; my kids weren't running off to school in mismatched clothes. But emotionally, the color had been drained out of my life. Nothing seemed to excite me. Then again, nothing set me off either.

Although Paul had crawled back into my life, the grayness also seemed to lessen his effect on me, too. Ativan made me feel less scared of being alone, so at the first sign that he was back on drugs, I showed him the door. Most of my life, I felt that living alone gave me no security at all; without a man I was nothing. But in my gray world, with no feelings, I didn't feel so insecure by myself. The tapping was gone, yet I was managing to live just fine. Ativan made manageable my overall level of general discomfort. I just felt . . . *nothing.*

My Virtual Life Online

I stopped taking Ativan all the time, and only popped a pill when I needed to leave the house. When I was in my room, lost in my cyber world, I didn't need it. I let the color back into my life, and I'd feel *alive* again. That computer had become my vice, my nightlife, and my bar scene. I began to wish that I could have color in my real life, too—or perhaps this was a yearning for the old familiar chaos. Maybe I wasn't so free from my cravings for the tapping as I thought.

Every now and then I would leave the safety net of the computer screen and tempt fate. I told myself that I just wanted to see how long I could last in the real world without throwing a pill under my tongue. Deep down, however, lurked the hope that I had finally been cured. I thought maybe the Ativan, given enough time, could drain all the *crazy* out of me. But my optimistic beliefs were always proven wrong. I would be out doing some normal activity and accidentally look up at someone. My heart would start racing and my muscles would tighten, and I'd know that I had lost. There was no cure. I was still crazy.

By this time, I had hidden in my room for so long that I no longer had friends outside of the online world I'd immersed myself in. Although my friends were now only online, for once they were people I felt I belonged with. I could talk for hours with this new group, and I never felt weird or crazy, or like I was going to die. With them I felt normal. I was "Heather," but I was normal.

The chat room where I spent most of my time was a mix of guys and gals from Canada and the U.S., most of them in their 20s and 30s. Everyone seemed to just be looking to pass the time. But some I could tell were looking for a bit more. I could tell that some were lying about who they were, like I was, but very few said anything serious that triggered my intuition.

My screen name was *HeatherUwish*—and it empowered me, making me feel like no guy was good enough. "You wish you could have this," was my new mantra. At least it was online. In any case, it was much better than my old mantra of "I'm crazy."

I thought my screen name could keep guys away, or at least show them who was the boss. It was all part of the new persona I had created—the one I wished I could be offline.

Despite hanging out in what was pretty much a "singles" group, I shot most guys down before they even had a chance. I had power in this online world, and I wasn't afraid to use it. It became almost a game to put the guys who flirted with me in their place. I still had a bit of a twinge inside me; I hadn't completely let go of my addiction to the tapping of chaos and danger. I could sense that old familiar pull whenever I got a vibe that maybe one of these guys was *bad news*. But we were online, after all; what harm could there be? We'd never meet. If I met someone from my online contacts, they'd know I wasn't Heather but crazy Carmel. I had no desire to blow my cover.

"Beautiful Day, Isn't It?"

Maybe it was being able to get a little fix of chaos online that allowed me to feel a bit more comfortable and courageous enough to get out of the house from time to time. Occasionally, I would wander out to the coast to enjoy the view of the Pacific Ocean. I would listen to the waves crashing against the rocks, powerful and unforgiving. The rhythmic sounds of the ocean had a way of calming my heart, making me feel peace rather than fear. As much as I loved my new group of friends online, from time to time, I just needed to be alone. Alone with nature.

I found myself sneaking off to the beach more and more often. Paul was gone, and I was still getting over the loss of my grandfather and the guilt of not being there for my mom. I felt like I could talk to Grandpa better there, although I didn't have any idea at the time that I actually *could*. I'd just drop my kids off at school, and on the way home my car would naturally drift toward the sea. There was one spot I always sat to quiet my mind and watch the waves crashing. People would pass by, but never stay. I was free from panic there, at least most days.

One day, I must have been sitting there for nearly an hour, so focused on my own calmness that I didn't notice at first the man who sat down next to me. The sea breeze was flowing through my now not-so-frizzy hair, and the sound of the waves soothed me, probably because they were louder than my own pounding heart. The man just waited for me to notice him. Although, I knew he was there, I didn't let on. I sat silently and waited for him to leave. I was too calm today, too happy, and too relaxed to lose my cool. I didn't want to have to go running back to my room.

I could see his big black boots out of the corner of my eye and smell the leather of his coat. *Biker,* I thought to myself, still ignoring him. I thought that deep down he was probably strong and controlling like Paul, yet I somehow felt calm and comfortable next to him.

"Beautiful day, isn't it?" he said in a voice much less intimidating than his footwear suggested. I lifted my glance as high as the bottom of his bearded chin. I was scared to look him in the eyes, wanting to hold on to my inner calm as long as I could. He was bigger than Paul, but not as big as my father. I expected to feel the tapping slowly caressing my skin, but the sensation was much fainter than I expected. I still felt it slightly, because I was scared of him. He was a man; that was enough to know to be frightened. Men control me and they beat me, of this I was certain.

At the same time, my intuition remained calm. I didn't get any red flags from him. Instead, I seemed to know that my fear wasn't justified. I realized that I had two options here, and I weighed them in my mind: the smoggy gray of Ativan, or the potential panic entering my life? As I lifted my eyes slightly higher to meet his bright blue eyes, I reached into my pocket and grabbed the pill. *Gray.*

"My name's Dave. What's yours?" His eyes were kind and inviting, not terrifying and crazy like Paul's. He was cute, too, a nice bonus. I spent the rest of the afternoon with him on that beach, and then I headed home. I walked into the house with a smile that I hadn't worn in years.

An Affair of the Heart

I'm sure Mom thought my good mood was from the Ativan, but I knew the difference. This time the peaceful happy feeling was because of *Dave*. He had a way about him that made me feel comfortable. At the same time, he made me want to risk the panic and be out in the open if it meant I could spend time with him. My mom thought I was turning over a new leaf, going out, meeting people, and cutting the cord that previously attached me to my computer. I never spoke a word to her of my new romance.

I was able to abandon my small online world every day for weeks to meet Dave. I made a new excuse to my mom and my children when they asked what I had done each day. I never told anyone the truth. I was still ashamed of my life, my past choices, and my mistakes with men. I felt as though they would look at this situation with judgment, first judging him and then judging me. I just wanted to be free for a little while longer, so I told little white lies to keep everyone happy. I'm going to the store. I'm meeting a friend for coffee. I'm going for a walk. It was easier than facing the shame and judgment.

I soon realized that I didn't need my Ativan whenever I was with Dave, although I still always kept it in my pocket. We would talk about everything and nothing. Before I knew it, I could feel myself falling in love with him. I'd never been with a man before that I didn't have to talk to all the time. With Dave, we could just sit and be quiet. I could feel myself beginning to let go. Maybe my heart was beginning to heal.

We talked and ate and made love like we were teenagers, but the whole time I knew my fear would prevail. I loved being with him. He was funny and kind and something about him made me feel like I was *home*. Not the childhood home I'd shared with my parents, but a home I had yet to find . . . a home where I belonged and I wanted to live in.

Dave had that badass biker exterior that matched so well with that persona I'd made up online—the girl I thought I wanted to be—but inside he was as soft as I was. He made me feel safe.

I left Heather at home, but I still kept a certain amount of distance between Dave and me. At least, I tried to. I told myself that I refused to fall in love. I had too much experience with fear to let love blossom in my life. I steadfastly refused to allow this to turn into a "relationship" because I knew those always ended in black eyes and broken hearts.

When I realized that my feelings for him were changing, that without him my day just wasn't as bright, I began to feel terrified that I had made a mistake. Strange how I seemed to associate love with bad choices. I was afraid to add to my burden with even more shame; God knows, my pile was already high enough. That's when I convinced myself I had to break up with him. Besides, he had responsibilities to go back to, a home and a job up north. I had to stay here with my four kids.

So when Dave suggested staying, I said no. I let Heather take the controls in my real life, and I broke up with him. Heather did what she wanted; she played the bitch, put up walls, and numbed the pain with Ativan. And despite all of his heart-filled attempts to keep me, fear won out. Again I made the choice to let go of safety and love.

A Life-Changing Surprise

I never really stopped thinking about Dave, unsure whether I'd done the right thing. But a few months later, as I sat in the doctor's office, I realized how bad of a mistake I'd made. I was zoned out, barely able to hear the words: "You're four months pregnant."

I truly felt numb. My oldest, Melissa, was nine years old, and my youngest, Emily, was six. How in the world could this be happening to me? I used protection . . . I was careful. My head was spinning.

It had been four months since I stopped talking to Dave. Four months since I broke his heart and forced him away, and now I would have to call and tell him *this*. I cringed to think of what I would say, dreading the conversation, wishing instead that I could retreat to my world of gray and hide under my pile of shame—which had just become a bigger pile of shame, decidedly bigger.

It took some time for me to get up the courage to make the call. The phone rang three times before he picked up, crushing my hope of getting an answering machine instead. The lump in my throat was so big, I thought I was going to choke. All I could muster up was a meek hello, but he knew instantly it was me.

"Carmel, I waited and waited for you to call. Why didn't you call me back? I wanted to be with you. Why didn't you call?"

I didn't answer. I just breathed softly into the phone, trying to find the words to tell him. I was holding on to some hope he might actually be happy to hear this news.

He continued, "When I didn't hear from you, I gave up, Carmel. My wife and I decided to try again, and now she's pregnant."

Now my silence was from shock. Those few seconds after he spoke seemed like hours as I contemplated my options. If I blurted out the truth, he might choose me over her. I knew it was likely. I knew he had felt what I felt.

I also knew from our endless talks that his wife had suffered a stroke years before. Now she was having a baby, and she needed him more than I did. She deserved him and so did that baby. I was too broken to love anyone anyway.

So I told him I was sorry I called, and before he could utter another word, I hung up. Then I did the only thing I knew how to do. I called the last number on my phone, the number that had been calling me five times a day for months, trying to get me back. I called Paul.

Back to the Love I Knew

Paul had been calling and begging me to come back since he'd broken up with his latest fling. The only difference now was that I felt like I had no choice but to take him back. What would people think of me if I had a baby alone? How could I have the baby of a guy no one even knew about, a guy who was now back with his wife and having another child? I quickly put together my own lies and built a story, covering the shame the only way I knew how.

Within a month of reconciling with Paul, I told him that I was pregnant. Just like every time before, he was thrilled. I'm not sure why it surprised me so much to see his face light up as I told him. I knew that Paul knew that this baby wasn't his; but Paul lived half in denial and half in truth. To him, this was just what we needed to rekindle our love and rebuild our marriage. He could live with the ambiguity of the date of birth.

It had been a long 12 years since we'd met in high school. We'd gone through so much together during that time. Yet he badly wanted to believe that I wanted him again. Just about as badly as I wanted to believe he had now changed. Who was trying to fool whom, you might wonder. The thought crossed my mind, but I quickly swallowed my concerns. I remember seeing him become a new man that day—whether he truly was or not is debatable, but I was certainly seeing a Paul I had never seen before.

Paul was much more supportive to me during this pregnancy than he had been through any others we had shared. The guilt was building up in me, knowing that I would have to raise this child under the shadow of a lie. I realized that this lie had grown so large, it was engulfing all of the people around me, and I didn't know how to stop it. Nothing would stop the shame anyway, so why not keep adding to it? The day this new baby was born, I'd just be adding one more gigantic lie onto the pile, and I'd be covering up the shame of my two-week romance at the beach. But Paul's faithfulness to me, supporting me in a way he never had before, made me feel like it was worth it.

It turned out that this pregnancy would be my most difficult, both physically and emotionally. I was diagnosed early on with preeclampsia—a disorder characterized by high blood pressure that can affect several organs of the mother. But more taxing than the preeclampsia was the emotional weight of the lie about this baby's conception. I prayed that this little baby would look just like *me*, so the world would not have to learn the truth. I would often ask God over and over . . . *Why? Why me? Why now?* I was always asking why, feeling sorry for myself, being the victim. That is until one morning when I got an answer to my questions.

I was sitting on the porch with a blanket wrapped around me, enjoying the calm air before all the kids woke up, when I heard a whisper: "He will do great things."

The voice was so clear, but when I looked around there was nobody there. I simply smiled. I knew who they were referring to, even if I didn't know who "they" were.

A New Kind of Family Life

"It's a boy," the doctors said, passing Paul the small body over the operating room sheet. Keghan was born by C-section, a healthy and happy 9 pounds and 3 ounces. Unlike the other kids, Paul treated Keghan like gold from day one.

I would say Paul treated Keghan like his own, but his own were not treated this well, not even close. The three girls were often ignored, and Wayne was blamed for everything, yelled at and bullied by Paul most of his life. Keghan, on the other hand, could do no wrong. Paul treated him like he was everything in the world to him.

Personally, I think it was because Paul knew. He knew deep down the lie that I had started, and he was trying to prove to the world that this was really his son. He was now hiding his own shame, his shame of a failed marriage that we were trying once again to make work, of a wife who had found another love, of a baby that wasn't really his. He was lying to himself to hide his shame, just like I was. We both had lots of practice, God knows.

My gray-washed world slowly opened up to color once again as I weaned myself off Ativan for the pregnancy. Once Keghan was born, Paul also let go of the drugs that had always ripped us apart in the past. We moved back to Alberta so Paul could find work, and what he found only fueled my hope. Paul joined his dad at a union job and started making good money. There was even, to my mind, an added "bonus": the job did regular drug tests.

For the first time, our family was doing quite well, notwithstanding the pile of lies we were balancing on. Despite the tapping having returned, I now had hope, and I used that to keep justifying the lies. I even remember thinking one day, *Thank God I stayed.* It seemed to me that all the crap I'd gone through had been worth it, because we really had hope to make it as a family. The abuse had stopped, the fighting was minimal. *Wow, this is all going to be okay.*

The hope remained high, even when we got a call out of the blue from Social Services. Ironically, they were not interested in our own situation, but rather asking for our help. Paul's brother's daughter had asked them to try calling us, hoping we could keep her and her siblings together. They had been taken from their parents' care, and Social Services now wanted to know if we would take temporary custody of seven of our nieces and nephews while their parents got their lives straightened out. They didn't have any foster homes big enough to take them without splitting them up.

If this call had come at any other time, we would have had absolutely nothing to give these seven children. As timing would have it, when the call came in we had bundles of hope to share and so that's what we did.

My life did a 180-degree turn that day. I was 30 years old, and suddenly, I had 12 kids in my house. My focus needed to be on my role as a wife and mother; I had no choice but to stay "plugged in." I didn't have time for anxiety. It was still there, but I learned to cope—to an extent. When your mind and body are that busy, there is less time to worry about being crazy. You sort of accept it, rather than putting so much energy into forcing it away or covering it up.

I started driving again and learned to manage my anxiety with quirky new ways of dealing with all the things that needed to get done. For example, at the grocery store, one of the kids would go from aisle to aisle getting groceries, and Melissa would handle paying the cashier with the debit card. All I had to do was push the cart, and focus on keeping the voices away by avoiding eye contact. I simply walked and stared into the cart.

When you're already taking care of so many kids, what's another one? One of Paul's nephews tried to run away from his mother, so he also came to live with us, rounding out our brood to a baker's dozen. I'd gone from a mother of 5 to 13 in just a matter of months!

Lessons in Love and Parenting

With so many kids, we were encouraged by Social Services to move to a bigger house in another suburb. Even with an extra eight kids, somehow we were able to manage it all and remain sane. We had lots of support workers in place, Social Services made sure to stay very involved, and I was plugged in and engaged in the whole big crew. Things were finally working out. It must have been hard on the kids to be pulled away from their parents, and I hope we managed to make it easier by providing them a home. Yet I think that the ones who benefited the most were my own kids—and me!

I took classes on parenting and enjoyed them so much. I started to put serious thought into child care as a profession. I enjoyed having a house full of kids as much as I'd enjoyed working with kids in the after-school center when I first met Paul. When summer came and all the older children were out of school, we decided to take a trip to BC; but it would be a real family vacation this time, no leaving Dad behind. We rented a 15-passenger van and piled our baker's dozen in.

We spent almost three weeks swimming and laughing—and, okay, there was some fighting, but we had 13 kids with us, so let's be realistic! Most of all, there was more love and laughter than I was used to experiencing on family vacations. It was like the rare glimpses of normalcy I had had when I was little, when Grandpa passed us peaches and Dad's mood was still good.

Just as those moments had to come to an end when I was a child, they would have to run their course now, too. Looking back on this time now, I believe that Spirit had a plan for me as well as for those kids. I was heading for something else, but this life lesson needed to come first.

It all started early one morning, as the kids were just starting to stir. As I sat down with my tea to check my e-mails and pay some bills, I realized it had been nearly a month since I'd sat in front of that computer screen. At one point, my online world had been the center of my universe and my safety net. This day, that same screen brought my world crashing down.

An e-mail had arrived from the mother of the seven children we'd taken in: "You think you're so smart, don't you? Well, I bet you have no idea that I had sex with Paul a few times, a few years back."

Now you're probably thinking: *Of course she did. Who hadn't?* And if this e-mail had arrived at any other time, I probably would have reacted the same. But this wasn't any other point in my life. I'd finally felt *free.* I'd thought I was finally free from the anxiety, from the pain, neglect, abuse, and cheating. At least, until now.

I knew this woman was just angry and lashing out at me. In her mind, I had taken her kids away from her. Still, I knew in my heart that she was telling the truth. I'm sure when she wrote those words, her intention was not to cause so much pain. She couldn't have known that my life was already balancing delicately on a big pile of my own shame and lies. Anything could have toppled it, and this happened to be the stone that did just that. That e-mail ripped my heart out and tore away the hope I had been using to hide the shame and the lies. Soon after, my big beautiful family would fall to pieces.

Paul came up the stairs behind me as I finished the last word in the e-mail. I turned and looked at him, confronting him with what she said. He didn't need to utter a thing; his face said it all. I knew. In that moment, I realized nothing had changed. Nothing would ever change. I had been standing on false hope that was now torn right out from underneath me.

Without that e-mail, I may have stayed with Paul. I may have died with Paul—maybe even *because* of Paul. She may have been trying to manage her own pain by hurting me; but in doing so, she freed me. Most importantly, she freed my children at the same time. She probably freed her own children as well. Because the truth was that Paul hadn't really changed. Inevitably, he was going to turn back into the monster he once was. It was naïve of me to think that her kids would have escaped that entirely, and I no longer wanted any of that for me or my children either.

Shades of Gray

Breaking Out of the Cycle

I cried for days. I couldn't function. I felt empty and lost, and I was back to feeling worthless. *I would never be enough, would I?* And then I had a new mantra to add to my litany: "I'm worthless." But it didn't replace "I'm crazy," it just lived with it. "Worthless and crazy": it was quite the combination. With it came a new and vicious hate for Paul that grew within me from that day on and slowly engulfed my entire being.

Panic set in again with a vengeance, and I reached once more for the Ativan, throwing it under my tongue, begging for the grayness to take over. I called Social Services, and I told them I was leaving Paul. I also told them I was having a mental breakdown. I didn't say it out of spite. I said it because *it was true.* All I could feel was pain and anger.

The children were returned to their families. The seven siblings went back to their mother, to a home where she would be closely supervised for many months to come and where she likely received the same parent training I had. I was relieved to see that she did change. She broke away from her abusive relationship and began to put her children first. It's a shame we couldn't have been closer, since in truth, she and I had actually gone through very similar problems. Our abusers had even been brothers to each other. But Paul's inability to remain faithful had placed an impossible block between us.

I look back on all that pain now with gratitude, but only because I know that everything happens for a reason. Perhaps my heart had to be broken so that those children could learn to experience forgiveness and love for their own mother. Perhaps this situation gave this woman a chance to prove that she had changed with her children in her care again. And perhaps, all of this had to happen for *me* and for *my* kids. Paul was never going to be the father they needed, and he would never be the husband I yearned for. He would always bring us chaos, and he would teach the kids to always want the tapping, just like me.

That woman saved us that day, and she doesn't even know it. It took me a very long time to realize this, but it gives me peace to think about it now.

Time for a Fresh Start

As for me, there I was alone again. Once more I failed at making my marriage work, at making my life work, at making my kids happy. I was still the girl that men cheat on, the one they beat, and the crazy person who everyone hates.

Like I had done so many times before when Paul would leave me on my own, I spent many hours in my room crying. Not because I missed him, although a part of me probably did. I cried because I had failed at making someone love me. I was never going to be normal. *Crazy and worthless . . . crazy and worthless . . .*

In front of the computer screen while the kids were asleep and the house was silent, I fell to my knees, bowed my head in defeat, and prayed. I hadn't prayed many times in my life, but when I did, it was always out of desperation. With tears streaming down my face, I prayed for a man to love me, to save me, to heal me.

I prayed for a man because I knew of no other solution. I prayed so hard my head hurt and my hands were soaked in tears. Then I got into bed and I kept praying, over and over: "God, send me a good man. Send me a man who will love me and treat me how he should." I prayed and prayed and prayed and less than 24 hours later, my prayers were answered. God sent me Reid.

〜◎ ◎〜

Chapter Nine

SEWING WITH THE THREAD OF LIES

I had fallen back into the lure of my online world again, and Reid showed up in our chat room with a voice that melted hearts. The chat room was a combination of voice chat and typing, but Reid almost always chose the microphone over the keyboard. The minute I heard his voice I stood at attention—much like many of the other girls, I'm sure. He soon became the main attraction of my online world. To add to his mystique, Reid was based in Okinawa, Japan, as an F15 fighter jet mechanic for the United States Air Force.

I didn't hesitate to click on his profile. The first thing I noticed was his picture with his shaved head—a feature I'd been attracted to since meeting Keghan's real dad, Dave. The cherry on top was that Reid made me laugh. I was in a dark, lonely place when Reid appeared in that chat room, and he managed to make me forget everything I had been through. He was such a refreshing change of pace.

There were other guys that I flirted with online, like Connor. It had become almost a game between the two of us: his flirting, me shooting him down, him trying again. He played as well as I did. Connor didn't take any shit either, and when his name popped up on the chat group, I knew the games would begin. But I also knew that Connor was all wrong for me. My intuition threw up all kinds of red flags, but that didn't stop me from playing. If anything, the potential danger was what kept me interested, since I was still sometimes tempted by the tapping of chaos.

Once I met up with Reid, I could sense he was different. Heather's quick wit seemed to have grabbed his attention, and soon we were talking all hours of the day and night. With Reid, there were no red flags, no tapping, and no fear. He had a way of making me want to tell him the truth, because he made me feel safe. So I didn't play games with him or push him away. At least, not at first.

Children, Children, Everywhere

My mom would have done it for me, pushed him away I mean, if she had the chance. She had been stopping by to help with the kids every now and then, and once again she was getting concerned about the amount of time I was spending online. "You need to plug back in to your family!" she began to chant yet again, and I knew she was right. And I did try to, on my good days, the days when I could leave my room. When the Ativan cloaked gray around me, I would play the role of parent.

I wasn't truly plugged in, though. I could sometimes manage attending Wayne's football games because they were outside. I could hide from people easier outdoors. I always had a place I could run to or walk away. But when I had to be inside a gym full of parents—like to watch Melissa cheerleading—*that* was nearly impossible. I would feel trapped. The more I denied the voices, the louder and stronger they became as they desperately tried to get me to hear them. When that happened, I just couldn't stop the voices or the feelings, and my old mantra came back: "I'm crazy . . . I'm crazy . . . I'm crazy . . ."

I loved my kids but I needed my online world so much more because there I wasn't crazy. The people in the chat room became my friends. Some of them had even started dating each other, but most were single. As Heather, I felt special, accepted, and normal.

We were all chatting in the main group not long after Reid had joined, talking about Debbie's kids and Reid's love of motorcycles, when Reid asked me directly, over the microphone, "How many kids do you have?" I reacted out of panic more than wit. I caught Wayne standing in my doorway, waiting to ask me a question. "One son," I said. It could have been any one of them standing there that day, but it happened to be Wayne, so that's the one I claimed to have.

I wasn't just embarrassed that I had twice as many kids as anyone else in this room while being nearly the same age as them, if not younger. I was most embarrassed about the fact that I raised those kids with a man who beat the shit out of me for over a decade. In this online world, I was finally strong. I was a bitch and I was in charge, and having five kids with an abusive husband was the opposite of strong. Heather would never have done that.

I never wanted to share the story of *why* I raised five kids with a monster. How could I tell them that I was too weak to leave, too addicted to the tapping, too worthless, and too broken? I was ashamed of my weaknesses, my flaws, my past, and more than anything, I regretted my inability to really be Heather. I was hiding Carmel among all this shame because I was too ashamed of who Carmel really was.

"I thought you had more kids, Heather?" Dixie said in her strong Southern accent. *Shit.* This could have ended just like the day of my royal lie to Mary and Beth. Dixie could have taken down my ridiculous story, just as my brother did when I was eight. But she didn't. I wish she would have.

"Yes, they stay with me. But they are my sister's kids, not mine. I just have one," I said. I was so consumed by my online facade, I didn't even think before I said it. Besides, I'd never see these people in real life. Our online and offline lives would never collide . . . or so I thought.

Real Life Meets Online

Reid and I grew so close we decided to meet. He took his first trip to Canada to see me, in fact, not long after I lied about the number of my children to the chat room. Only a few months after that first visit, we were announcing our engagement to the kids. Much to my excitement, they seemed to love Reid as much as I did.

Of course the kids had come up in conversation between us, sometimes in such a way that I thought Reid must have known the truth about them. But he never pushed me to tell him that they were all mine out loud, and so I never did. He was as deeply in love with me as I was with him, and he wanted nothing more than to take care of me and to be with me in person, not just through a screen.

Shortly after one visit, while we chatted on webcam, he got down on one knee and asked me to marry him. It wasn't at my favorite Chinese restaurant this time; it was much better. As odd as it might seem to others, he was proposing to me in the one place I felt normal, comfortable, and not crazy: *online*. When I was with Reid, I not only felt lucky that he picked me out of all the other girls, I felt empowered by him as well.

The kids loved Reid instantly; they were ready to have a real family built on love. While Reid was heading back to Japan, this time we'd all be going with him. The kids were thrilled by this news, and it was amazing how seamlessly Reid stepped up to become a father figure to them all. In fact, Keghan, only three years old at the time, just walked up to him and said, "You be my dad, Reid?" It was as if he picked him.

At this point, Keghan didn't know that Paul wasn't really his dad. He wasn't even old enough to really remember when Paul lived with us, but it was almost like he instantly knew Reid was a better choice. Reid was honored to step up to the plate for Keghan, and they became best buds within no time.

The wedding was small but full of love. My parents weren't there, but we were joined by all our kids, my sister, a cousin, and some select friends for our ceremony on the beach. As I said those vows, for the second time now, I wasn't thinking of the past. I wasn't recounting all the times these vows had already been broken. Instead I was thinking only of the future, wondering if Reid would still take me in sickness (and in *craziness* and in *shame*), not just in health.

The lie about my children wasn't the only thing I was holding back from Reid as we boarded that 747 to Okinawa, Japan, just a few days after our wedding. Our mostly online relationship had allowed me to keep my panic and anxiety a secret from him as well. When he visited me in Canada, I always chose to eat in our hotel room rather than a restaurant. I told him it was better because we'd have more time alone. It was the truth, too; with him, I just couldn't get enough time alone. But there was more to it, as I knew only too well.

As time went on, the excuses continued, the same excuses I'd been using most of my life. I told him I didn't like driving because it stressed me out. I said I didn't work because of the kids. I didn't tell him that I'd been on social assistance for years because my extreme panic attacks didn't allow me to work. I relied heavily on my mom and my cousin to help with the driving and day-to-day tasks.

Too Many Spirits, Too Little Space

As we boarded that plane, I had to let one of my two lies go. I'd only had to take one step onto the plane when I knew; this was going to be horrific. My heart pounded uncontrollably, my muscles tensed, and my legs began to shake. I could see Reid's fear for me increase each minute along with my own terror. He comforted me the entire flight, getting me ice, rubbing my back. I could see the genuine concern in his eyes. He was nearly as scared for me as I was for myself.

When the tires screeched onto the runway, Reid bolted awake. He had fallen asleep rubbing my back only a couple hours earlier, and he rubbed his eyes as he checked that I was okay. I already had my things together and was itching to get out of that seat, out of the tin box full of people and full of thoughts, anxiety, and panic.

The Ativan had worn off by now, and I'd had a female's voice in my head for the last hour of the flight. She was saying to tell her daughter that it's okay she never got to say good-bye, that her dad needs to eat more, and the house should go on the market in June! She would not stop talking. I tried to ignore and deny this voice, the way I always did, but the intensity of my physical symptoms was increasing. The pulsing pains in my chest now were so close together that I only felt one deep pain. It felt like I might not even make it. As I walked out into the hot muggy air, I was relieved. The panic would soon subside, and the pain would drift away. Or so I thought.

You would think, with all the time I had spent on the Internet over the years, I might have done a bit of research before moving across the world to a country I knew nothing about. I'm pretty sure that if I'd bothered to find out the population of Okinawa, I would have thought twice before packing up my family and moving to such a small island crowded with so many people. But the population wasn't the only obstacle I'd face when I landed in Japan. Because I was unaware at the time of any link between Spirits and my symptoms, I couldn't have known how bad Japan would be for me, a country where the dead are buried *aboveground.* There are memorials with people mourning their loved ones all over the streets. There are not graveyards tucked away like we have in North America; a memorial can be anywhere.

I'd see people praying or mourning and feel intense anxiety. I'd hear all sorts of voices that I knew weren't mine, I'd feel emotions out of nowhere that made no sense to me. I was struck with sadness and grief one minute, and then feel like I was having a heart attack the next. And there was no escaping this.

I thought that the city was going to kill me for the few months we lived off base. I couldn't avoid the triggers; they were absolutely everywhere. Reid knew I was a wreck any place in public, so we rarely wandered far from home. When we did, I would beg to go back, afraid of the panic.

Once we had made it to the confines of the Air Force Base in our four-bedroom military home, we hardly ever left. I didn't dare. We did have to make some trips outside the gates, but only when my panic was so bad I was convinced I was dying. Reid took me to the hospital a few times during the period of time we were there. Of course, the doctors I saw in Japan found no physical problems and offered no cure either. No one could. Apart from me just being crazy.

I struggled to keep myself distracted, but I could see Reid's worry change to confusion: *What could be wrong with my wife?* He always wanted to help me, and I think it pained him that he wasn't able to. No one knew quite what was wrong with me. As time passed, the panic attacks came less frequently, but I was never one of the outgoing and social Air Force wives I met. I did make a couple friends, but mostly I stayed at home a lot.

Reid had been in Okinawa for four years already by the time I moved there with the kids. Within a year of us arriving, it was time for him to move on to his next posting, which turned out to be England. I didn't want to go to England; it was another small island full of people, another version of Japan, and I just couldn't take it any longer.

Tempted to Find the Tapping

After much discussion, Reid decided to apply for something called "force shaping" to see if he could be released early from the military. I don't think we even waited three weeks after he applied before he came home to announce that it had been approved. They were letting him out early. I didn't know where I was heading, but I knew I was ready to go—a feeling my kids didn't share.

The kids had absolutely loved Okinawa. Wayne took up skateboarding, and I think he can tell you every single part of that island he skated at. He met lifelong friends there, and for the first time in his life, he knew the love of a dad. Melissa was just reaching her teenage years when we arrived in Japan, so that was where she first discovered boys—a discovery that kept Reid on his toes. Jessica and Emily had lots of friends, and they'd settled into school and military life with ease. But it was Keghan who had the closest relationship with Reid. Keghan would watch for him to come home every day after work. He would even dress up in his little uniform and pretend he was Reid. The kids were happier than I had ever seen them. Reid was happy and I should have been as well; but I wasn't.

Reid's love for me and his selfless devotion to our family was so foreign to me that I didn't know how to react to it. In the past, love had always been mixed with chaos and tension, so I had learned to always remain guarded even with those I loved the most. I knew men could love you, could make you feel safe and feel wanted, but I also knew it didn't last. In my reality, the more a man got to know me, and the more he learned of the truth— my craziness, my anxiety, my weirdness—the faster that this love would turn into the love I'd always known.

I was waiting for Reid to yell, to scream at me, to hit me, to shove me to the ground, but it never happened. I waited for that switch to flip every time we came back from the hospital, every time I didn't clean the house, every time I survived another panic attack. I waited for a reaction I was sure had to be coming soon, because it always did. But it never came. When my skin didn't pulse and the comfort of the tapping never appeared, I did the only thing I knew to do: *I went searching for it.* My addiction had grown so strong that I needed the chaos more than I needed the peace.

We hadn't even begun packing up our house—we'd be moving to New York, close to Reid's family—when I decided to uproot my life. The lie was weighing me down, and I wanted to tell Reid the truth of the kids, the truth about *my* kids. I threw the words at him plainly: "I lied. The kids are all mine. My sister didn't die."

I waited for the bomb; surely this time he would explode. I waited for the tapping to reappear and for him to send me packing. I was almost ready to get up and leave before I even said it, I was so certain of his response.

He looked up at me, still buttoning up his uniform . . . and smiled. "I know," he said. He hugged me. And that was that. No chaos. No explosion. Just love.

I should have felt lighter then, with one less lie on my pile, but all I felt was the absence of what I thought I needed. I was feeling it even more intensely now, because I knew that there was probably nothing I could say that would bring the chaos falling down around me. It was so strange. I hardly knew what to think.

Can Love Overcome the Addiction?

In New York, Reid's family greeted us with open arms and more love than any of us could have ever imagined. They were over the moon that Reid was finally home, and even happier to have gained five new grandchildren. Reid's family was perfect; at least, they would have been for a person who understood how to love without chaos.

Reid's father loved his children in a way I couldn't begin to understand, but I was envious of nonetheless. When Reid's dad looked at his own daughter and told her how proud he was of her, it made me want to stay with them forever. He put her on a pedestal as the only daughter, but it was a pedestal so different from the one my dad had made for me. My dad loved me with money, and the few warm moments I remember with him were so rare and so long ago.

But I felt Reid's dad's love for me, too. This man poured his heart into making us feel at home now that we were a part of the family. I felt like I had become his daughter overnight. Their entire family accepted us all without any hesitation. Keghan and Reid were still best buddies. All the kids, for the first time, had a dad and an extended family that treated them the way they deserved to be treated. There was no tension in Reid's parents' home, and there was no tension in mine now, either.

But try as hard as I could, I didn't know how to live that way. I used to wish I could have stayed in that home forever. If only I could have quit the chaos like I did cigarettes, cold turkey. But this addiction of mine was deep in my soul, and I just wasn't ready to live without it yet. All the love and warmth in that family couldn't have cured me because I felt powerless to the allure of the tapping.

Therefore, as the love grew in our new home in New York, so did my fear that it would all come crashing down. I sabotaged our beautiful lives, determined to keep the tapping alive, by taking the bricks out the foundation one by one, ensuring that the walls would indeed come crashing down around us all.

Chapter Ten

UNABLE TO LOVE

Our home in New York was beautiful, and our idyllic street felt like it could be out of a Hollywood movie. We hung a Canadian flag on one side and an American flag on the other, with a wicker rocking chair out front on our white veranda. Reid's family helped us renovate, and by the time we were done it was perfect in every way. To me, it was picture-perfect, like our family. This time, it was more than just appearances—we *were* a picture-perfect family. Wayne joined the high school football team, and the kids all made friends more quickly than I'd ever managed to. They were all so happy to have a family, to have friends, and to finally have a real dad.

I spent my days at home, but this time it wasn't because of fear. In this small town, with so few people, I was surrounded by nothing but love. I did all of the things my mom had been trying for years to get me to do. I cooked, I cleaned, and I hung the laundry outside on the clothesline that Reid's dad had hung for us. And in the process of it all, I was beginning to heal.

The only problem is that in order to truly heal, you first have to *feel*. As I felt the old wounds of my past slough off, all of the pain and anger was revealed, like the layers of an onion. As I made my way down, one layer at a time, the pain of my past was exposed, and I began to relive the chaos.

With every layer of pain that Reid and his loving family peeled off, I could feel my addiction to the chaos grow stronger as well. It was eerie. I acted the way most addicts do: I put myself, my addiction, above everyone else. I didn't think about the family that had taken me in, who had shown me nothing but love. Worst of all, I didn't think about what it would do to my kids. I selfishly thought only about myself and the chaos that I'd always known; the chaos I needed in order to feel normal. I was determined to find it and I got creative.

Desperate for a Fix

First, I convinced myself that Reid thought I was fat and that he didn't love me; I wasn't good enough. I convinced myself he couldn't love me, because love was a TV flying at my face or torn tendons in my arm. I convinced myself that I had ruined his life by making him raise kids that weren't his, but even more so, by making him live in my lies. This wasn't love. It couldn't be because there was no chaos in it. And once I was done convincing myself, I set out to convince Reid.

I reverted back to victim mode, but this time I didn't want to be saved. I retreated to my lonely, gray life despite Reid's every effort to save me. I pushed him away and clawed at our beautiful life, tearing down the walls of our home, one lie, one fight, one accusation at a time. Over and over.

I unplugged from it all. I went back to where I always went when I could no longer handle the world around me; I turned on the computer. Among these lies, in this imaginary world, I could be happy. It's the place where I had only one child, where I was the one in control, the bitch who didn't take any crap. But this time I wasn't escaping chaos, I was *looking* for it.

The minute I logged on to my old chat rooms, I was looking for trouble; and I knew just where to find it. Sure enough, Red-flag Connor was still there, and he jumped at the chance to play the same games we used to play. My intuition told me he *was* the chaos; he *was* the tapping; he *was* what I knew about being loved.

This time, however, when I pulled him in, I didn't chew him up and spit him back out. I was no longer Heather talking to Connor; now I was *Carmel* desperate for a fix. I let the conversations online turn into texts and eventually into phone calls. The phone calls would turn into arguments and fights, followed by forgiveness. I'd catch him flirting with other girls online when I'd wake up in the middle of the night unable to sleep. He'd deny it all to me and tell me I was crazy, calling me names I'd heard come from Paul's mouth. I'd found what I'd been subconsciously looking for. *The tapping was back.*

I was back in the cycle Paul had taught me, the one I learned from my parents. While I sat in a house of love, peace, happiness, and safety, I *chose* chaos over safety once again. This time I chose Connor over Reid.

Initially, I clung to my relationship with Connor as my only chance to hang on to the tapping, to breathe in the chaos of dysfunctional "love" that was so familiar and so real. Gradually, I started believing that this kind of love was the only kind I deserved. I didn't deserve the love that Reid and his family had spoon-fed me selflessly for months. I felt like a feral cat that someone had tried to take in the house. I didn't deserve to be happy, and I most certainly didn't deserve to be free. I turned back into the 15-year-old girl with a black eye and shattered arms. I was convinced I was worthless, and someone this worthless could not be loved. *I could not be redeemed.*

A Return to Broken Dreams

When I told Reid I wanted to go back to Canada because I could no longer be his wife in New York, he said okay. That's all he said, but the way he sat in that chair across the table from me, I knew that he was angry. He didn't even look at me. I knew he had already let me go. He was done fighting for me. He was done trying to convince me that he loved me or that I was worth it.

I was acutely aware that Reid's anger wasn't anything like Paul's or my dad's when they were mad. Reid didn't hit me or spit at me; he remained calm. His quiet acceptance made me feel even lower than the beatings and the warm spit dripping down my face. This time I felt low because of what *I* had done, because deep down I knew this breakup was all my own doing. Reid couldn't understand because he didn't know how badly I was broken. He never understood the tapping, and the power it had over me; then again, at the time, neither did I.

We told everyone I was just going home for a bit to visit my family, but we all knew that was a lie. I could see the pain and anger in Reid's eyes as he took me to the airport and knew that he just wanted this all to be over. When I walked into that airport, I felt like an addict about to get a hit. I could almost feel my drug entering me. From the very first fight Connor and I had, only minutes after he picked me up at the airport back in Canada, I knew I was *home*. I was back amid the chaos and the kind of love I thought was the only thing I really deserved.

A few days after I'd met up with Connor in Edmonton, I called Reid. He had told his family the truth, and they were completely devastated. He told them the lie about the kids, he told them everything. Now at my request, my kids had to pack up all of their things and say good-bye to the only solid father figure they had ever known. I was dragging them right back to the chaos they were born into—all except for Keghan. Keghan was the only one of my kids who had never lived in that chaos, and now I was forcing him into it. I was so sick, so ashamed, that I tore him away from the only man he ever loved as a father and forced him to live my addiction with me.

Reid sent me money to get myself settled before sending the kids, and I rented a house outside of Edmonton with Connor. When I first met Reid I was so mindful to ensure my two lives did not collide, that I was a mother first and a woman second. I'd been so careful to ensure that I didn't let Reid know my kids until I felt he could be completely trusted. But here I was, setting up a home with a man that I *knew* was an awful choice. I felt so drawn to the pain he offered, I was too sick to even consider what this would do to my children.

I was so ashamed of who I really was, so busy hiding the real me, I didn't even know who *me* was anymore.

Sorting Through the Mess

There was no physical abuse this time, but the yelling never stopped. As far as the kids were concerned, I had basically just moved them back in with Paul. The kids were furious with me for uprooting them from New York, and they started to rebel. Not only had I torn them away from their perfect, happy, and *safe* lives, but I had done it right in their pivotal years, when they were becoming young adults. They should have been learning how to put down roots and build trusting friendships; instead they had to start over in a new school and with a tyrannical father figure at home.

I found out very soon into our relationship that Connor had bipolar disorder or something of the sort; there was no wagering what mood he would be in or when he would erupt. He was like a loose cannon, very much like my dad when I was young. I did my best to try to keep him happy, which wasn't easy. Connor didn't like the kids and had no patience for anything they did. The messes they made, how loud they would be, the fact that he couldn't do whatever he wanted anymore—it all annoyed him.

Obviously, it didn't take me long to realize I had made a huge mistake. And when I did, I picked up the phone and called Reid. I told him I loved him and wanted to come back, but I had hurt him too much already. He was rightfully still angry with me for leaving him, for taking all of the love he gave me and tossing it out the window. He didn't yell—he never did—but he didn't come and save me like he would have before. I'd burned that bridge.

Until that call, I had been living only in my own selfish world. But when I put down the phone that day, I fully realized the devastation I had caused to Reid and what I had done to my kids. I was finally dealing with the consequences of my actions. It was such a shocking and painful personal revelation that I couldn't bury it again.

Reid called me back a few months later. He wore his heart on his sleeve as he told me that he still loved me, that he could move up to live with us and we could start again. This time, however, I was the one who said no. Not because I didn't want to, or because

I didn't love him, because I still did love him very much. I said no because I refused to hurt him another time. I knew by then how strong my addiction had become and how blind it had made me to the world.

I mourned Reid for a long time, but there did come a day that I was finally able to forgive myself for hurting him, for hurting the man that I believe God sent me to teach me what unconditional love was.

Trying to Make My Life "Work"

As much as I didn't trust myself not to hurt Reid more than I already had, I also didn't know how to be alone. Within weeks of that phone call, I married Connor. A quick ceremony with a justice of the peace, another set of vows that I had come to know only as lies, and an extra side of shame. I married Connor to hide the shame of being alone, of being a girlfriend rather than a wife at my age, of being a single mother with five children. But truth be told, I was just as ashamed of marrying him as I was ashamed of myself.

We didn't tell anyone about getting hitched in the apartment of the local justice of the peace. If that doesn't scream shame, I'm not sure what does. We did eventually tell my kids a couple days later, and had a party in our backyard to celebrate, only to wake up the next morning with Connor in yet another rage.

When the kids and I settled back in Canada, it didn't take me long to figure out that, like Paul, Connor didn't like to work. He was a pipefitter by trade, but it was hard to tell since he never worked steadily. He wasn't happy to be the sole supporter of a family. So I did what was expected of me and found a way to go back to work. I decided to start my own business and opened up our home to the only thing I knew well: *children.*

I started a home daycare, which brought some very nice perks to our lives. It put food on the table and it kept me busy, and it also kept us in one spot long enough for my own kids to make some decent friends. Although my anxiety was never far from my mind,

I was back in a city that I knew well, and I had all the rules of how to manage my anxiety down pat. Better yet, with this job I could stay home all day, and when the parents came to get their kids, it was generally only one or two adults in my home at any given time. One or two, I could handle.

Then one day one of the mothers of the children I took care of came pounding at my door. "Come, come!" she yelled in pure ecstasy. Melissa, who often helped out with the kids, followed me, wondering what all the fuss was about. The young mother dragged us both out to the driveway.

"Look what my new fiancé bought me!" she said as she pointed to a sparkling, pearly-white Denali parked in my driveway. "Isn't it beautiful?"

I stood speechless as I stared at it. It was gorgeous. It was the nicest vehicle I'd ever seen, and her new giant engagement ring nearly blinded me along with it. After I finally tore my eyes off the dazzling finish of her new car, I looked over at my own car, one I'd bought after Connor's truck got repossessed. The car was old, and most days it sputtered and struggled to start, usually because I'd only managed to scrounge up a few dollars of gas to get me home.

As Melissa and I watched the Denali drive out of our driveway and past my piece of junk on the street, I looked at my daughter and said, "I'm going to have one of those one day." Melissa turned around to go back in the house, not even taking note of my comment. I didn't move though, watching the car drive off. "Mark my words—one day I'll have one."

That day lit a fire beneath my ass. I no longer saw my home daycare as just a means to pay the rent; it became a chance to get ahead. I brought in a few more kids and began taking it quite seriously. It raised my confidence when I realized what a success my little business had become. All of the mothers and fathers were constantly expressing their gratitude to me, as if what I was doing was a favor to them. I don't think they realized that *they* were the ones doing *me* the favor.

As my confidence grew, my patience with Connor wore thin. Connor's patience with me must have been quite short as well, because he was taking more and more jobs out of town. I still had chaos in the form of the fights we'd have whenever we talked on the phone, but at least we could breathe. Our house began to breathe just the way my parents' house did when I was young—tight when Connor was home, free and easy when he was gone. I was truly in my element.

Letting Someone Else Decide

With Connor out of town all the time, I became quite good friends with Allison, the wife of one of his friends. I had a lot in common with her, and she had a set of twins that my kids just loved playing with. Allison and I talked about raising children and how I could deal better with Connor; she even pushed me to leave him. "Every man you have ever picked has been wrong for you," she said to me. "Why don't you let someone else decide, for once?"

I wasn't sure I subscribed fully to her words, but they did make me think. Perhaps I *was* incapable of choosing the right man. The more of a jerk Connor became, the more she would remind me of why I needed to get out. Then one day, she decided to take the matter into her own hands altogether. She thought the only way I would leave Connor was if I had someone to leave him for, and it just so happened she had the perfect person in mind.

I told her no, but deep down I yearned for someone else to take the reins of my life. I wondered if maybe she was right—maybe someone else could make my own decisions better than I could. I had a pretty dismal track record after all.

She set me up to meet this guy at a casual dinner at her house. Then at the end of the evening, Allison made up an excuse as to why she couldn't drive me home and asked him to take me. On the way home, he asked for my number and insisted on taking me for dinner. He was an incredibly kind man, and as I sat there deciding what to do, he told me he could see I was broken, and he just wanted to show me love. I probably should have said no. I should have thanked him for the ride home and said good-bye—but I didn't.

His name was Rob, and he was a big man like my dad. He was strong, smart, wealthy, and attractive. He worked as a welding inspector and was always traveling. Before he left for his next trip, he asked that I let him take me out on a date. He called me and e-mailed me the next day to insist: "It's just a harmless date."

A harmless date, eh? I didn't even know what that was. First of all, *harmless* couldn't even touch this situation, because I was still married. Not only that, I was still crazy. After a conversation with Connor, who had only called me to yell at me for the color of the sky, I called Rob back and said, "Yes. Please take me away."

A Fairy-Tale Romance

Using the word *away* here turned out to be a big understatement. Rob took me to whole new world I'd never known. We went to a beautiful restaurant, where he held the door for me, pulled out my chair, and doted on me all evening. On that first date, as I looked at him staring lovingly at me, I realized that nothing would be the same again. I was going to fall in love with this man; I knew it that moment. And I did, more quickly than I'd ever fallen in love with anyone before.

When I was with him I felt like I was floating, like his world revolved only around me. Finally, I was the daughter of the queen of England. Rob was looking for a trophy wife, someone to take care of and spoil, someone to stand by his side. I was happy to take that role, not because he forced me to, but because I wanted to. I wanted to be a princess, and I wanted Rob to be my Prince Charming.

He had only a few weeks left in Canada before his next work trip to India, and it just so happened that those two weeks coincided with Connor working out of town. Rob wanted to spend as much time with me as possible, and he made it hard for me to refuse. He knew how worried I was about my car breaking down, so he would always come pick me up. He'd often offer to take me to Allison's so all the kids could spend some time together. Then on Rob's last night before his trip to India, we spent the night together at his hotel. I knew I was cheating, but lying in bed with

Rob that night, I felt that there was nothing from the past holding on to me. I wanted nothing but to stay with him forever.

During the short time Rob and I had spent together, my anger toward men seemed to have already drifted away. Perhaps the lessons from Reid had finally stuck. The biggest difference between my relationship with Reid and with Rob was that I never tested Rob. Allison had chosen Rob, and Allison was healthy—at least she was healthier than I saw myself to be. I concluded that Rob was a better choice than any other choice I had made before, because I trusted Allison so much more than I trusted myself.

Since I didn't have to doubt myself, I dove head first into love with Rob—no fear, no tapping, just love. Rob loved me with nothing but kindness, just the way Reid did, but this time I believed him. "I want to be with you," he told me. "I'm falling in love with you. I'll take care of you, forever."

The truth was that he was already taking care of me. He took care of me both financially and emotionally. He helped me to get a new car and sent money to help with my bills so that I could leave Connor. But he didn't just love me with money, like my dad had done when I was young. He told me he loved me constantly and made me feel more loved than I had ever felt before. For the first time, I allowed someone to love me the way love should really feel, without pain.

When Rob asked us to move in with him, I didn't even hesitate. Not long after he left for India, he gave me access to his accounts, gave me a budget of half a million dollars, and told me to buy us a house. I had no idea how to shop for a house with that much money; I had never even heard of that much money! But within ten short days, I found the perfect place. We communicated over e-mail for the remainder of his trip, and by the time he was back, we had our new home, fit for a queen.

I had found my Prince Charming, and my kids were now the princes and princesses. They didn't have to lie to their friends anymore. They could walk around in brand-name clothes, and when they needed extra money for their after-school activities, I could just say yes; I didn't have to count pennies. But better than all that, my children had a family with two parents, with love and without chaos. Rob had bought me the most beautiful promise ring, the kids had dirt bikes and any toys they could want, and our world had turned completely around.

One day, when Rob got home from one of his many trips, he told me my car needed an upgrade. He took me to a car dealership, walking me straight to a beautiful black Denali. *"This* is what I want to buy you!" he said. He had never known, but I did—*I would one day have that car.*

Following My Intuition

My life with Rob was so perfect, I questioned it from time to time. I would call up Allison and ask her, "What am I missing? What is wrong with this guy, this can't be real can it?" She would assure me that life was finally good. I knew deep down she was right, because there were no red flags. My intuition was saying the same thing as Allison; this guy really was the Prince Charming I thought he was.

He cooked me dinner, helped with the kids, carried in the groceries, opened doors, pulled out my chair, and treated me with love and kindness. He would say, "It's my job to take care of you." This was something no one had ever told me before. This was what heaven must be like, I thought.

My life had become so stress-free and easy that I'd even managed to get my anxiety under control. Now that I had money, I also didn't have the added financial worries. I got the kids to pay with my bankcard when we'd go shopping, so I didn't have to engage with people at the register for too long. I'd only go into restaurants that had booths so that I could keep people out of my eyesight. I could never do lines, whether in a store or at an event; but then again, I never had to. Rob was a gentleman and always offered to stand in line for me.

When I look back at this point in my life, I remember everything as being perfect. One day though, it all changed. I'm not surprised that it happened, I'm just surprised that I never saw it coming.

Rob was confirming his next itinerary for his business trip to Brazil when Wayne asked him if he wanted to go outside and try his new quad bike with him. When Rob left the room, I sat down in front of the computer screen to check my bank account. On the screen, however, Rob's e-mail account was still open. I could see details about the trip he'd taken to India almost a year earlier.

I began reminiscing when I saw it; that trip had been right after our magical night in the hotel near my house. I thought back to how strong my love for him was from the very beginning. Then I felt a twinge from my intuition, something I hadn't felt for a long time. Something inside me said to look further. As I read the itinerary something didn't add up. Edmonton to Toronto. Toronto to Thailand. Thailand to India.

Thailand? Why would he be in Thailand? He never said anything about being there, all he said was he would be in a "remote area" of India with no contact for ten days. Surely Thailand isn't that remote? Why didn't he tell me about Thailand?

And Love Comes Tumbling Down

The questions piled up in my mind, and I felt the need to know more. I scrolled through his e-mails, looking for an explanation. What I found was a conversation I did not want to believe was true. A friend of his had written to him: "Here is the place I was talking about in Thailand. You'll love it. Have fun at the Sugar Shack."

I heard a voice in my head say: "Look at his pictures." And that was it. My perfect life and love was gone, crumbling beneath me, one photo at a time. I flicked through picture after picture of my perfect Prince Charming surrounded by women in a Thai brothel, and I broke into a thousand pieces.

I didn't understand his reasons for going to Thailand to find romance when he could have stayed with me in the hotel. To be honest, that thought plagued me for many years. *Why wasn't I good enough?* Cue the nervous breakdown.

Looking back on this now with more compassion, I believe that when he left for Thailand, he was in love with the idea of me, but he was not yet in love with me. When I found out about the brothel, it had been ten months later, and he had fallen in love with me since then.

My kids never knew what I saw that day on the computer. Rob spent hours convincing me it was a mistake and he was sorry, but I couldn't hear him. All I could hear was the chaos and the pain of my own past. This is when I went to the deepest, darkest place I think my Spirit has ever been. I retreated into my room and cried for weeks. I no longer wanted to make love to Rob; all I could think of was him with other women.

Emotionally, mentally, and physically, I unplugged; once again, I had gone completely numb. I was still there for the kids and did my best to attend to their needs. I got them to their team sports, school dances, and other activities, but my head was elsewhere. It didn't take me long to fully immerse myself in the victim mentality, and by the time Rob left for his business trip to Brazil, he was leaving a completely different woman than the one he had met and fallen in love with less than a year earlier.

At this point, I was no longer Carmel. I wasn't even Heather. I was just plain broken. I know now that Rob didn't deserve it, but I wanted him to pay. Not just for his one mistake, a mistake that didn't even compare to the mistakes that I or my other partners had made, but still I wanted him to pay for it all. And he did.

Rob paid financially and emotionally for every man who ever laid a hand on me, lied to me, cheated on me, abused me, or stopped loving me. He paid for them all. And then he paid for the shame of my anxiety and panic. He paid for everything I hated about myself. I blamed it *all* on him.

When he left for Brazil, I went straight to the mall. Shopping had never been something I enjoyed because of my anxiety. There were always way too many people around, but today I was searching for triggers, and Rob's bank account paid the price. I was on a mission of revenge. I should have just left Rob, but that's not the person I was then. I was too broken to be logical. So I hurt him, just like I hurt Reid and Chase. I spent Rob's money, then I left him.

But I did pause long enough to ask myself an uncomfortable question: "I wonder if men are the liars here—*or maybe the liar is me?*"

Chapter Eleven

FINDING MY LIGHT

In order to find myself this time, I retreated within myself whenever I could. I wanted to forget about Rob, Connor, and Paul and my whole lifetime of ill-fated choices. I let the darkness of the evening take over my life. I went out to bars, not looking for a connection, but rather for an escape. I let myself get so dark, so far from control, so deep in the tunnel that I was almost blinded when the light at the end shone in my eyes.

It was brilliant. The light. *My light.* I stopped dead in my tracks and stared into those blue eyes, ones I vividly remembered from the first time I saw them on the beach. I remembered feeling warm, selfless, and safe with a man for the first time in my life and being too scared to let it take root. Now here he was again. It was Dave. *Keghan's dad.*

"Carmel!" Dave yelled over the music. "What are you doing here?" He was as confused as I was to see him in Edmonton, nowhere near where we first met. We were now hundreds of miles from the spot where he stole my heart and left me with a gift I had never told him about. At that moment, I stood there in shock; I couldn't move. The lie I'd told him came crashing down over my heart with so much force that the panic and anxiety overtook my body. All of that emotion and shame came flooding back, and I felt again like I was dying.

"I've been looking for you for years!" he yelled, grabbing me and wrapping me up into a huge hug. He told me that he and his wife had separated long ago, and she'd moved to another province.

He now lived in Grande Prairie, which wasn't too distant from Edmonton, where he worked as a heavy-duty mobile mechanic and owned a bike painting business. He also told me that he was raising his little girl, Mikaela. She was the baby his wife had been carrying when we'd previously spoken on the phone, the news that made me keep silent about my own pregnancy.

"Give me your number," he said. "I can't lose touch with you again! Are you single? Can I take you for coffee?"

I continued to stare at him, feeling stiff as a board, struggling to make any words come out at all. I managed to get out, "It's a bit complicated."

Finding the Best Way to Fess Up

I left the bar, numb with the panic and anxiety that I'd staved off until that moment. All of the shame and the lies I had blamed on the men in my life, all of the pain that I made Rob pay for, came flooding back now—it was all *my* shame, *my* lies, and *my* chaos. It all came back up with this one lie that had been hidden so deep, it blew a hole in my soul as it came back up. *Dave had no idea he had a son.*

When I got home, I went to my room. I cried and prayed and cried some more. "Get me out of this, take me out of all the lies. I just want to heal. I just don't want to be crazy." I prayed over and over, until I could pray no more. My lie resurfacing made me realize that while I had tried to protect Dave and not tear his marriage apart, I had instead hurt him as well as my own son.

Seeing Dave made the full force of my panic and anxiety come flooding back. Maybe Spirit had decided I was done feeling sorry for myself. It was time to get back in the game and live up to my past. But I couldn't do it by myself. I needed help. So I did what my mother did the last time the anxiety took over my life. I opened the phone book and picked the first name on the page of counselors. After all, I was crazy and it's their job to help crazy people, right? I asked the therapist to clear an entire day for me. "An hour won't be enough," I assured her.

It took me the entire daylong appointment to lay every one of my lies out on the table. Every tall tale I had ever told came out, all the shame and half-truths; I didn't even mention the voices. After all, I wasn't sure I was quite ready to be committed.

The therapist looked at me in shock, but also with compassion. "When you left Paul, you were suffering from post-traumatic stress disorder from all his physical and mental abuse. You turned into a bulldozer, plowing over everything that came in your path," she said. "You have to find the truth of who you are and the truth of a life that you want."

The pile of lies was so big, I didn't even know where to start to find my truth. She offered to help me take the first step: Have Dave come in, and we would tell him together that he had a son he didn't know about. She made it sound easy, but I was still a wreck.

Finally Breaking the Big News

When I called Dave that night, he was ecstatic to hear my voice. I had avoided numerous calls and texts from him long enough that he thought he'd lost me again. "Can I finally take you on that date?" he asked.

I told him I would go out with him the following week, under the condition that he first come with me to see my counselor that week. "Just an hour," I said, thinking that would likely be the last time I saw him, if he even came.

I was terrified, thinking of how my lie would affect him. I didn't expect him to say yes, especially not as quickly as he did, laughing at my absurd request. But I figured the date would never happen—and I never wanted it to anyway. I just wanted to get rid of that lie, one of so many.

As Dave sat down with me in my therapist's office, I wasn't sure how to start. As both Dave and my counselor stared at me, I knew I had to just do it. As I let the words fall out of my mouth, I could see the tears fall, one by one, down his face. Finally, I finished revealing a secret that I had kept buried so deep, it almost seemed as if I were telling a story about someone else entirely. *What kind of monster am I?*

I told him that I was *so* sorry, but I knew sorry just didn't cut it. I didn't know how to make up for the pain I caused him, and my heart ached inside. But then I heard the sound of laughter, and noticed Dave's body moving with the noise. His smile grew so wide that I realized that his tears weren't tears of pain, but tears of *joy.*

"Finally! You'll never get away from me now!" he said, which put an immediate look of concern on both my face and on the counselor's. Then this leather-clad, tattooed biker smiled with his damp cheeks and confessed his love once again. "I have been in love with you and trying to find you for seven years! That's why you called me that day, isn't it?"

"She's not dating you, she just needed to tell you the truth," the counselor piped up, taking the words right out of my mouth.

"Oh yes she is. She owes me a date and I'm getting it, and more," he insisted.

And damn, if he wasn't right about that.

The Beauty of Consistently Showing Up

Dave let go of his business and moved to Edmonton to be closer to me and his son. He told me all the time that one day I would marry him. I was terrified, though. At first I refused to hold his hand, to let him take me out, to let this relationship go anywhere except co-parenting. My understanding of men was that they cheated on me, beat me, or gave up on me—and if they didn't do any of that, all I could look forward to was breaking their heart. I wasn't ready to go through that again, so I did my best to keep him at bay.

But Dave was persistent. In fact, he still is. He would always ask me how he could prove to me he was different, that we were meant to be together. "Just admit that you love me!" he'd say, but I kept denying it. I told him what love was. I told him the movie *The Notebook* was love. That leaving someone and still loving them was true love. Never cheating, never beating, living so selflessly to forfeit your own happiness for someone else was love. But that love didn't really exist. It was only a movie, of course, so we could never have that. *Why should we even try?*

But he continued to show up. He never gave up on me. He hung out with the kids as much as he could, taking the boys to hockey and coming over for barbeques with them every weekend. We introduced him to the kids as my friend, but I think he had them convinced that we should be dating even before he managed to convince me! And one day, he did manage to. It was the day he showed up with a pile of letters, wrapped in a bow, each one addressed to me.

And along the bottom of each envelope, he wrote: *If this letter ever becomes undeliverable, return to the Red Lamp Post.* This was a place we had agreed to meet should one of us die before the other. When he gave them to me, I immediately remembered the letters Noah wrote to Allie in *The Notebook,* forgetting I had even told him what that movie had meant to me. He told me that if I ever doubted his love, even for a second, I should open the letters and read each one. There were 365; I counted.

Today this stack of letters sits on my shelf in my reading room. I've never opened them, and they are in the exact same bundle I got them in on that day. Because I know, just by looking at the stack, he loves me as much as Noah loved Allie. I never need to read them; seeing them is enough to remind myself of his love.

We didn't marry right away, though. A wedding wasn't high on either of our lists of favorite things to do. We had both already done that three times, followed by three divorces, and we agreed it wasn't necessary. Instead we had a commitment ceremony and celebrated our new family—finally together. But that doesn't mean our love affair was a completely smooth one.

Trying My Best to Re-create the Chaos

"Just leave me, then, why don't you?" I yelled at Dave as I smashed a porcelain ornament against the wall.

"Well, that was three bucks down the drain," he responded, smirking. "Why don't you throw another? I think that one over there looks good!"

Dave didn't get mad. Like Reid, Dave had this way about him that seemed to always keep him calm. But unlike Reid, Dave knew everything I had gone through. He knew what I was doing. He knew I was still healing from my past.

"I'm leaving! You don't love me," I'd yell, still waiting for him to explode. But he'd only laugh, just like the day I told him the giant secret about Keghan.

"Carm, you are having a mini freak-out," he'd reply, so calmly that I sometimes wondered if he'd even noticed what I'd just done. "This is where you try to push me away, and I don't leave. I love you, so I am going to the store, and you're going to work through this little freak-out. When I get home, everything will be okay."

I'd scream and yell and throw some more things, but when he'd get back, I was calm, just as he predicted. I'm not sure how he knew how to deal with me, but he did, and thank God for that!

This whole relationship was a new experience for me—standing up for myself was new to me. I felt as if I were caught between two extremes. On one end of the spectrum, I felt I had to control absolutely everything to make up for all the control I had given up to men in my past. But somehow I still kept one foot straddled all the way on the other side, also trying to please everyone.

I still wasn't sure who I was, who my authentic self was, so I continued to be who I thought the people around me wanted me to be. I was trying to take the reins of my own life, but I wasn't able to give myself the love I needed yet. Instead I followed my old pattern and kept trying to find that love from everyone else.

Struggling with Control Issues

I didn't just control the ups and downs of the relationship between Dave and me, I also started to take control of the group of friends Dave had before we moved in together. He and his friends rode motorcycles, and the whole idea of that lifestyle made me uneasy. So instead of telling him how nervous I was and what my fears were, I decided to join it and try to control it.

I invited Dave's friends over to our house and went above and beyond to make sure everyone had a good time, feeding and entertaining them to no end. We had his friends over so often, they became an extension of our family. Soon they became my friends as well, and I spent many hours just gossiping with the girls. The kids thought it was the coolest, given the leather-clad characteristics of our new "family," but at the same time, it was still a bit chaotic. This wasn't who I truly was either—but I didn't know that yet. I let that new lifestyle envelop our lives. I even got a tattoo that said, "Property of Dave." Of course, I made *him* get a matching tattoo!

As I got used to having Dave's friends around, I also gained a fair bit of control over my panic and anxiety. But there are certain things in life that you can't control—particularly when it comes to your kids.

"I'm pregnant," the text from Melissa declared.

That little shit! I thought. *Pregnant at 18.*

Well, I'd heard it said that the apple doesn't fall far from the tree. Melissa and I were very close in more than just age. Now we had one more thing in common.

When this news broke, a part of me was angry. I was mad at myself more than anyone. I hadn't, after all, broken the cycle. My daughter, like my mother and me, became pregnant in her teens. I thought I'd given her all the tools she needed. We had "the talk," she had birth control, she had all the knowledge, I knew all her friends. I worried what this would mean for her, for her education, for her future.

After a while, the worry faded, and I became more happy than angry. A part of me knew it was a good thing, but a part of me felt guilty—as if I had been the cause of this. If only I hadn't moved her around so much, or if only she had a better relationship with her dad, or any father for that matter. I searched for answers and tried hard to embrace what would be, hoping she would make it through this okay. I took it in stride and we soon embraced the surprise. Now I am ever so grateful for my first grandson, Ben.

Facing the Fears of a Health Scare

When I received a call from Mikaela's school, our lives would take a different turn out of our control. A teacher was asking me to bring a new pair of pants to the school for her. "Did she fall down?" I asked, wondering why on earth an eight-year-old needed me to bring her a new pair of pants.

"No, she didn't," the teacher said, hesitantly. More annoyed than alarmed, I found her a pair of pants and got in the car. About halfway there, my phone rang again, and this time the urgency was clear. Mikaela had wet herself, they said, and was not speaking to them. "She must be embarrassed. You need to hurry."

When I got to the school Mikaela—Mike, as we call her—had her head down, and she didn't move as I called her name. When I reached her, I lifted her chin to look her in her eyes, and in that instant I knew—something was very wrong. I remembered that Mike's mom had suffered from strokes and yelled at the school staff, *"Call 911, now!"*

When Dave found us at the hospital, I knew from the tears streaming down his face that he had seen this before. A few hours and several exams later, the last thing we expected happened; they were sending us home from the hospital. The symptoms seemed to have gone away the same way they appeared, slowly and with no explanation whatsoever. They told us that Mike had something called hemiplegic migraines and not to worry. We would schedule a test for those in a few weeks, they said.

When we got home, though, I knew there was something more. Not like I knew what Mr. Thompson was thinking—but a gut feeling that all moms have. Something just wasn't right. Mike had become a daughter to me as fast as my kids had all become Dave's kids. The worry I had felt for my children when Paul would storm in the front door was the same worry I was feeling now for Mike; it was the same helplessness, too.

"What's four plus four, Mike?" I asked her, waiting for a response as she stared into space at our kitchen table.

"I don't know," she said.

How could she not know? A few hours later, I asked the same question but this time she looked right at me, as if I were crazy.

"It's eight, of course!"

Mother's Intuition on High Alert

Three days after Mike had been rushed from school to the hospital, I was on the phone with a nurse, crying and begging to get Mike in for an MRI sooner. I was not sure why the nurse took my word—maybe she had dealt with mother's intuition before—but I'm sure it saved Mike's life.

Before Mike was even out of the MRI machine that morning, we were surrounded by specialists of all sorts. We knew our lives were changing again as Mike was wheeled out of the MRI on a stretcher. That's when the panic set in. It wasn't the panic I was used to, although my heart was certainly beating as fast as it did every other time. This time I didn't think I was going to die, I was worried Mike might be the one to die—and according to the doctors, this wasn't just a random fear but a real possibility.

Mike was having a stroke. In fact, she'd been having one all weekend, from the time she'd been rushed to the hospital on Friday to now, Monday morning. It took days and a long string of tests to finally diagnose Mike with Moyamoya disease. As much as it sounds like a lovely Hawaiian BBQ dish, believe me—it's nothing nearly as pleasant.

One day Mike had been jumping on the trampoline, laughing and smiling, and the next she was in the pediatric intensive care unit, unable to move her right arm or leg, and communicating only with her left hand. She was barely able to open her eyes at times. Mike needed brain surgery, but they couldn't operate until the stroke stopped and her brain had, to my understanding, "cooled down."

Dave needed to keep working, so I moved into the hospital nearly full-time with Mike. Dave came by every day after work, while Melissa and Jessica took shifts at home helping out with the mom duties and stopping in to help me in the hospital when they found the extra time.

A Hospital Full of Spirits

While I spent more and more time in the hospital with Mike, my fear only intensified, as did my panic and anxiety. I spent so much time in the hospital I was beginning to think that I, too, needed brain surgery. As it was, I was also forced to come to terms with my situation, to realize that I was still broken myself and my intense anxiety was still with me.

While Mike healed I kept my focus on her, on keeping her alive and on keeping my panic at bay, at least the best I could. I took the stairs and avoided the elevator at all costs. We didn't need a repeat of the last time I was in an elevator! I would shut the door to the room to "keep it quiet" and left her room only when it was absolutely necessary. When I just couldn't take it anymore, Melissa would come and take over for me—at eight months pregnant, she was nearly bursting at the seams! I did my best to push the panic away, but it never stopped showing up. If anything, it got harder and harder the longer we were there.

When the doctors finally gave Mike the thumbs up for surgery, I was relieved not only for her health, but also to know that soon we could leave this place of fear that was closing in around me. The surgery had only been done four times in Canada, and it involved taking Mike's brain, turning it upside down, and then reconnecting it. At least that's the way I can most easily explain it to you. I couldn't help but think while they were describing it to us, *Maybe that's what I need, too.*

The morning of Mike's surgery, sick of sitting awake in the dark, I quietly snuck to the bathroom to start my morning ritual of brushing my teeth and washing my face the best I could in that awkward sink. But before I could start, I heard a little voice call out, "Mommy?"

I turned my head, wondering if it was Mike I was hearing, even though it sounded as if the voice were coming straight out of the sink drain.

"Mommy!" the voice came back, louder and now completely terrified.

I ran out of the door to get to Mike, only to find her and Dave still fast asleep. I returned to the bathroom, scared, confused, and unsure of what I had heard. The air was so cold. I felt a shiver run up my spine along with something I'd never felt outside of my body before. I gave up my attempts at my morning ritual, and just got out of there as fast as I could.

Freaked out and not sure what to think, I woke up Dave and Mike to get ready for the surgery. I never spoke a word of that to anyone, but I knew in that moment that something was wrong. Thank goodness, the surgery went smoothly and Mike was soon able to leave the hospital.

Just as we were leaving, suddenly Melissa was phoning us— labor pains! Back to the hospital we went, this time bubbling over with happiness. We were so excited to welcome our first grandson into the world.

The Joy of New Life

Melissa named her son Benjamin David, after his grandpa. He was a joy in our lives after the stress and fear of Mike's illness. Ben couldn't have arrived at a better time, and as I looked into his smiling face and beautiful eyes for the first time, I realized that Mike was not the only one who needed to heal. I did, too. I needed to heal to be the mother, grandmother, and wife I knew I could be. One without fear, without anxiety, and without "crazy."

Mike's health scare and Ben's arrival made us think differently about our family. We realized that the biker-rally commitment ceremony wasn't really going to cut it. Marriage was about more than just vows now. That legal document also came with the right to make life-saving decisions, should anything happen to either of us. We needed to have those rights, to have guardianship over each other's children. And so, we got married.

It was a very small, sweet wedding in the backyard. We had the kids, a few friends, and Dave's mom around us as we made it legal. For once I felt like the words we were saying to each other were *worth* something. They weren't just vows, they were a real commitment; not just to each other, but also to our family and our kids.

When the excitement of the last-minute wedding wore off, I was left with the feeling that it was time to face the panic I had vowed to deal with that day I heard voices coming from the sink in the hospital. Since then, my panic and anxiety had been on the rise again. I fought my desire to retreat into my own world away from people and even away from my family. But I knew that wouldn't really solve things. This time, I would keep on searching and keep on trying, determined that somehow, I would find *a way to fix myself.*

☙ ◉ ◉ ❧

Chapter Twelve

MY HEALING JOURNEY

I didn't know where to start with this elusive concept of "healing," but I suspected that I needed to retreat from all of the triggers and look within myself for the answers. I had a few close friends but, for the most part, I disconnected myself from the other people in my life. Rather than staying home to gossip and cook with Dave's biker friends the way I had before Mike's surgery, I began spending more of my time alone. I read self-help books in my search for answers, trying to get my anxiety under better control, once and for all.

Sure enough, I chanced upon the next big step in my healing journey on a day that started very much like any other day. I was out picking up groceries one afternoon when I stumbled upon a store called Gifts and Other Things. It sounded to me like the kind of place that usually has only one or two people in it, the type of store that you can saunter through for as long as you want without seeming too weird.

I went in and walked slowly through the aisles, looking at the different trinkets and books. I realized that the objects in this store were things I had never seen before. It was full of strange-looking gems and stones and books on witchcraft, Spirits, Angels, and other topics I had never even thought of. They even had a wall full of decks of cards that I had no context for; I only knew them to resemble what psychics used at the county fairs. It was really quite fascinating.

After wandering around for some time, I decided to buy a couple of candles—just about the only thing in this store that I knew how to use! But as I stood at the counter, waiting for the cashier to wrap them up in tissue for me, a book sitting next to the register immediately caught my eye. On the cover were the two words that had been ruling my life: *Panic* and *Anxiety*. I picked it up to look at it, and as I did, the cashier took notice.

"Do you have panic and anxiety?" she asked, to which I just nodded in agreement. She continued her casual chatter as she rang up the purchase. "I believe that all people who have panic and anxiety are psychics," she added.

I stared back at her rather blankly. *Psychic? Me? If that were true, you'd think that maybe I would have known enough to skip the first three husbands!* I laughed to myself, thinking of what an absurd thought it was. *Me. A psychic. Now that would really be "crazy."*

She suggested that I get a reading and handed over two business cards: one for an Irish intuitive healer and one for a medium. I was intrigued, so I put them in my purse and walked out of the store with my candles, still questioning the woman's strange assumption that I might be some kind of psychic.

Seeking Clarity about My Own Path

Curiosity kept stirring me up inside and by the time I got home, I had decided to take her advice. I dug out the business cards from my purse and called the first one I looked at, which was for the Irish healer. Terrified as to what she was going to do, what crazy things she might tell me, I brought a friend with me and made her get a reading first. While I waited for my friend's session to finish, I picked up a book up off the coffee table and began reading the first chapter.

"We are each responsible for all of our experiences," the first line said. I kept reading. "Each one of us decides to incarnate upon this planet at a particular point in time and space. We have chosen to come here to learn a particular lesson that will advance us upon our Spiritual, evolutionary pathway."

I was more and more intrigued. *Maybe I'm not crazy!* I became so overwhelmed with emotion as I continued to read this book. Tears were streaming down my face by the time the healer came to get me. It was my lightbulb moment—the moment I first realized that, if I had chosen this life, then I was not crazy. *I was just learning.*

The Irish healer opened me up to the reality of how people do energy work. One of the most important things I learned was that it was safe and natural to get a reading or healing done from a practitioner such as this. I was quite surprised that she knew about a few specific health concerns that I struggled with; my symptoms were not visible and they weren't anything she could have researched. Her knowledge convinced me that it was possible for a person to just "know" things. In fact she mentioned that I had been dropped out of my carriage as a baby, something I didn't even know about myself. But my mother confirmed it later when I asked her.

What I most remember from that day, however, was the book that I'd started to read in the waiting room. The minute my session was over, I ran out and bought that book with the big heart on the cover, *You Can Heal Your Life* by Louise Hay. I slept with it under my pillow and read it every night before going to bed. I still use this book today and follow its guiding principles.

With the help and guidance of this book and others, I began to let go of my past and forgive the people who had hurt me. I had to after all, since I was the one who had actually chosen them to be close to me in this life. Once I began to forgive, I also accepted my past and began to doubt the belief that I had carried with me for so long that I was "crazy."

But this new idea of "choosing" our own lives, our own lessons, and our own paths piqued my curiosity. I wondered about Spirits and souls, and one question kept looming over me: *Could I really be psychic?* What if the woman in the store was right? If this was true, maybe I could use my own inner knowledge to get rid of the panic and anxiety that continued to plague me. So I dug out the second business card and called the medium to set up an appointment with her.

The medium began our session by handing me a deck of cards and asking me to shuffle them. When I gave them back to her, she pulled a card. She looked down at it, then looked up at me, and said without hesitation, "I see you are a medium."

I was quick to set her straight. "Uhhh, no . . . I'm not."

She looked obviously confused, but I felt certain. Being psychic was something that *maybe* I could accept. Knowing things about other people sounded useful. But to be a medium who speaks with dead people? *No way!*

"Yes, you are," she said. Her tone was authoritative. It wasn't the one that people use when they're trying to prove someone else is wrong; it reminded me of the tone that my father used to use when he knew, beyond a shadow of a doubt, that he was right.

The medium and I talked about my anxiety, the panic attacks, and the voices. Each time I told her something new, rather than looking at me as if I were nuts, she looked at me as if she already knew.

"What you are feeling around you are Spirits. Until you learn to connect with them, you will always feel this anxiety," she said.

Now that was truly a revelation. I walked out enlightened, but also a little defiant. I didn't want to be a medium. I didn't want anything to do with dead people. *Maybe she made that up,* I thought. *Maybe she meant to say "psychic."* But I had to know for sure.

I went back to that shop with the strange-looking objects. This time, I selected a book by Sonia Choquette, a world-renowned psychic and author from Chicago, called *Diary of a Psychic: Shattering the Myths*. I devoured it, soaking up everything she said. This was the first time I'd ever read anything like this, yet at the same time so much of the information seemed so familiar.

From Sonia I learned so much about what was really going on when I would get those feelings and that inner knowledge. She explained that I was using my sixth sense. Sonia was quite convinced that we all have an inner sixth sense, and the more I read, the less crazy I felt. I realized that I had a lot of the same childhood experiences that Sonia did when she was a child, I'd just chosen to deny it. No one in my family gave me any bit of encouragement or understanding, whereas Sonia grew up with a supportive mother who taught Sonia to embrace her extra-sensory gifts and abilities as completely normal.

Reading at the Kitchen Table

While I resonated so much with Sonia's story, there still seemed to be a whole lot I needed to learn, so I went back for more. I bought more books by various psychics, more books by Louise Hay, anything I could get about auras, Angels, and Spirits. The all-or-nothing girl in me came out, and I became instantly addicted to finding out more and more about this whole new world I never knew existed. With this new thirst for knowledge, I began pouring in lots of time and money to learning more. Soon I was also buying crystals and candles. Then I even built an altar in my home so I could display these new treasures.

I bought a set of oracle cards, similar to the ones I saw the medium use when she did my reading. I found out that oracle cards are used for all sorts of things, not just for fortune telling, and while they are similar to Tarot cards, they're not quite the same. Oracle cards can be used for astrology or any sort of spiritual guidance. The cards come in different sizes, with different numbers of cards in each deck. The ones I enjoyed looking at had pictures or artwork on each card, and most had a small description on the card as well to help the individual using the cards discover clues to the past, present, or future.

Opening up the box of my first set of cards, I remember feeling really excited but also a little nervous. I wondered if using oracle cards was anything like the Ouija board I'd heard so many scary things about. I had no idea what to do with them, but they seemed to fit so naturally in my hands as I shuffled them from one hand to another.

I skimmed through the little guidebook that came with them. The pages contained descriptions of each card to help you interpret the images. I had the urge to try them out on someone else, so not long after I purchased them, I gave them a try with my best friend.

As I flipped over one card at a time onto the kitchen table, thoughts began to come into my head. I had no idea what I was doing, but when I looked at the pictures on the cards, I would begin to interpret what that picture might mean. It was almost like I was using my imagination, but somehow, my imagination was right. I started speaking without even thinking, telling her the things I was feeling and that I somehow "knew," and the words just kept flowing out of my mouth.

I know what you're probably thinking, because I was too: *She's your best friend. Of course you know everything about her!* However, I knew more in-depth things than I'd ever known before. It was as if I could "feel" her feelings. I got a better sense of her emotions and knew a lot more about situations in her life than I had known. It was like when I could feel that Mr. Thompson didn't just hate his job, I even knew how he hated tuna salad—I just *knew* it somehow.

It was not the same as when I heard the voices, which were clearly coming from someone else. The thoughts in my head were still my own thoughts, but somehow, *I knew more.* It was like the knowledge was coming from within me. My sixth sense was tingling.

Could I Do It Again?

As powerful as this first experience was, it still wasn't enough to convince me. My friend's nephew sat next to her, and I asked if I could try this out on him. I didn't know much about this young man and thought it would be a better test of the cards to try them in less familiar territory. He was game, so I asked him to shuffle the cards the way the little guidebook instructed. When I took the deck back from him and started flipping cards over on the table, once again words started coming out of my mouth. But this time they were things I couldn't have possibly known, or guessed for that matter.

As I looked at this young man, I suddenly felt a veil of sadness come over me. It was as if I could feel his emotions. He was sad and just wanted to go home, back to the province he was from. I felt it the same way I felt Mr. Thompson's frustration with his wife. My friend's nephew didn't say a word as I spoke. He hadn't told anyone how homesick he was, and I could see his face frozen in shock as I let his secret out into the open. Tears welled up in his eyes as he stared at me

That's when I came to a realization. The impressions I was getting here at the kitchen table were coming into my head in the same way that the voices and impressions came to me when I was in high school. Then it dawned on me that these were the style of voices I'd heard when I spoke to the People in my body. They were the same voices I heard in high school, the same voices before every panic or anxiety attack. Now, for the first time ever, I was hearing these voices and I *didn't* feel like my heart was going to beat right out of my chest. Here, in my kitchen, during this reading, I didn't feel like I was going to die. On the contrary, I almost felt calm. The more I spoke, the calmer I became.

Suddenly, so much of my life made sense. I thought back to my five-year-old self in my room staring at my bull-teddy. I realized that in that moment, I had been the most authentic me that I had ever been. I blissfully spoke to the Spirits, and naturally discovered a way to incorporate them into my life to help me. But as I'd matured, I had drowned out that smart young girl and her natural gifts with layers of shame and lies.

Now, sitting at this table, the truth was coming back to the surface. I was learning who I was, moving cautiously but surely into my own authentic truth. And all this was happening because I was *listening* to Spirit instead of *denying* it.

A Reading with Too Much "Truth"

I was on a high that evening. The next morning, as soon as Dave came in from working on his bike, I beamed with excitement and waved him over. "Come see what these cards can do!" I shouted. He stopped halfway to the bathroom, still covered in grease from his bike, and sat down at the table next to me. I could tell by the look on his face that he wasn't really interested, but he could also see something new in me. So he humored me. He sat down, took the cards as I passed them to him, and shuffled them with his greasy hands. As soon as he passed them back to me, I placed a card on the table face up.

As I looked at the card, I could feel something come over me. It was like what I'd felt the day before when speaking to my friend's nephew. I can only explain it as a very serene feeling, as if you'd just walked into a peaceful setting. I experienced a sudden calmness and complete truth. I knew instantly when I saw the first card that Dave was mad at me. The card told me that he was angry, and I somehow also knew it was directed at me. I didn't say anything just yet; I just flipped another card onto the table. That's when I knew *why* he was mad.

The picture on the card told me his frustration was over finances, but again—I just *knew* more. He thought I was spending too much money and that I wasn't contributing to the household. As these thoughts came into my head, I began battling between the calm and peacefulness that is my connection to Spirit and the shock and disbelief that he was so mad at me. Yet he hadn't said a word! It was like there was a veil of truth that had come over me, and I couldn't alter or change the reading in any way, despite wanting to. I couldn't help but hear the truth. Still I bit my lip, incredulous, and wishing I could deny it.

Then after the fourth card was lying face up on the table, I was completely unable to hold back the words. I didn't say them nearly as calmly as I could have, though. "You are mad at me! You think I am spending too much money! And you feel all the financial burden and stress!" I blurted out, struggling between anger and peace.

Through gritted teeth, I continued, "You need to tell me how you feel. When you do, I may be mad, but I'll work more on helping." I was fighting every single word as it came out of my mouth, yet somehow the message was still coming through with love and compassion, just the way his Guides intended. Even though my brain, all the while, was screaming, *"No."*

No, I don't spend too much money! How dare he think this! What a jerk! I could feel my brain struggling with itself and insist that I should defend and justify myself. But try as I might to speak my own piece, those words my ego was screaming at me, all I could seem to say out loud was what the cards were telling me. *Nothing but truth came out.*

I stood up, swept the cards back into my hand, and shouted at him, "I am going to try to spend less money, and work at helping to support our family more!" Right before storming out, I managed to yell at him, *"And I'm never reading you again!"*

As I stomped off to my room, Dave stood up with a look of shock, clearly thinking, *What the heck just happened?* But we both had just heard a truth that needed to be said that day. And since then, I've been true to my word and have never given Dave another reading. Lesson learned! Psychics should not read for their dearly beloved without any warning or reason. And this was the first of many lessons on my road to enlightenment.

But before I could take on any more lessons, I had to face the reality that had just surfaced. It was my turn to step up to the "truth" that had come out. I was determined to find a way to contribute financially to this big, beautiful family unit. I also knew that I had to do it while living my own authentic truth because for the first time, while working with these cards, I had felt a kind of peaceful bliss that I wanted more of.

$\sim \textcircled{c} \textcircled{o} \sim$

Chapter Thirteen

LESSONS IN LIFE AND LOVE

It seemed like I was finally back at school, but this time it was on my own terms. I was learning something I was passionate about, and I could teach myself most of it through practice rather than having to worrying about elevators and classrooms. So I chalked up the troubles of my first and second readings to inexperience and was eager to learn more. The first lesson learned: Don't give readings to your husband—and I can tell you that was a pretty powerful message to myself. But the second lesson was even more profound: *You can never lie to anyone when you're connected to the Other Side.*

It's a strange job knowing you can't lie, but you simply can't speak anything but the truth when you work for the Other Side, because the messages coming through are from a place of love and light. Even though I was mad at Dave, I couldn't help but say what I did; the message was as much for me as it was for him. The truth was, I did need to contribute more. But more important than that, I needed to realize that this world I had been fearing my whole life—that had been causing me to lie to cover my shame—was nothing but truth. I had lied enough in my life and all I wanted now was *truth*. The Truth of Spirits and Truth of Carmel! It was all coming together. *Finally.*

Dave had every right to be mad at me for spending too much. I was shopping every day and spending so much on crystals, books, and cards that I hadn't really stopped to think what it was doing to our finances. I just had to have it all whenever I began a new idea or "thing." I was spending thousands on courses. And although both Dave and I were taken aback by the accuracy of the cards, we proceeded to avoid the topic altogether and never spoke about the reading I did for him or my temper tantrum that accompanied it. But I don't have to tell you that not talking about something rarely makes it better.

Starting to Develop My Gifts

The fact was that I was changing, and Dave saw that the change was good, even though he didn't understand it. I was so busy trying to understand it myself that I just kept immersing myself into the world of Spirits and readings, and Dave kept on the same path that he was always on, spending time on his work, his friends, and his interests. So Dave worked on his bikes, and I worked on my intuition. We were both happy, growing, and learning, but we were no longer doing it *together.*

"You're getting calmer, Babe," he'd say to me, happy to see me able to relax. But at the same time, he wasn't sure why it had happened. I'm not sure he wanted to know either—especially not if it meant another session with those cards!

He was correct that I was becoming calmer, and at the time I wasn't really sure why it was either. All I knew was that I was much more relaxed, and I could feel myself healing. I would try to explain things to Dave, but his own fear kept him from wanting to engage. I had hid the shame of my anxiety for so long that, as I was healing, I didn't want to hide anything anymore.

Now I really wanted to share all my excitement with Dave. I was finally starting to care less and less what outside people thought, which also meant I was starting to let all the shame slough away. *It was about time.* I wanted everyone to know about this new exciting life that was opening up to me.

Well, I was telling *almost everyone,* but I think perhaps my mother was the exception. She was the one person I'd always wanted approval from, and I still did. Moms are the type of people that we never stop trying to please, and I wasn't quite sure I wanted my mom to know about this new world of being psychic and using oracle cards to tell people the future. So when she came to visit, I wasn't certain how I would explain what I was doing, but I knew I had to eventually tell her.

Not Just Another "Hair Day"

You know what, I don't think Spirit thought I was opening up about my news quickly enough, because I suddenly got a big nudge from the Other Side while my mother was sitting right there! Here's how that day unfolded. While she was visiting, I brought her along with me to my best friend Sandra's house for a hair day. Lots of girls were going, and I thought it would be a fun "mom and daughter" day out. We were all visiting and talking about our families while Sandra's son was getting his haircut, and then Jade, who was one of the hairdressers, started telling a story about her dad.

I asked Jade how long it had been since she saw her dad, and she told me that her dad had passed away three years ago. I heard a voice inside my head. It was a man's voice, and not just any man's voice; I knew it was Jade's father. I felt as though my head had split in two, as he somehow managed to interrupt my own thoughts when he spoke. "Tell her I love her," I heard him say.

Shit! I thought. I immediately panicked. I'd just heard a dead person. Something was different. This wasn't like reading the cards. I knew I shouldn't have been playing around with those damn cards. I was sure I had somehow brought on a curse or played with the wrong kind of black magic. I just wanted to be a good psychic, to heal myself, to get rid of the panic and anxiety; I never wanted to talk to dead people.

"I told you, tell her I love her, right now!" Jade's father said in a forceful and desperate voice, this time louder and very stern—it almost made me shudder in fear.

I felt the blood drain from my face, and I instantly felt sick. What should I do? I was scared of saying anything, because somehow I felt that by responding—even in my own thoughts—I would be acknowledging that I was crazy. I had read so many books where the authors described using your intuition and how Guides can speak to us saying things that we wanted to hear, such as answers to our own internal questions. But this was not at all like that.

I'd thought from my readings that messages from Guides were loving and inspirational, appearing in dreams and meditations, a soft epiphany coming to you like a gentle breeze. And the books on Angels said the same. I had often heard Angels' messages while writing in my journal, and those sentiments were highly spiritual and full of love.

At my friend's home, watching her son get his hair cut, I was so confused because the experts and authors I followed hadn't said a word about *voices yelling at you in your head*. When you get messages from Angels and Guides, you were supposed to feel as though you have control of your thoughts, but in this moment I had lost all control. This was definitely not the gentle, loving, sixth sense that Sonia Choquette was talking about. *This was a dead person!*

In the Midst of Becoming a Medium

"Can you hear me? Tell her I love her! Right *now,*" the voice yelled one more time in my head, and I just wanted to get out of there. I wanted to run away and hide from it, but I was scared I would never get rid of the voice. *What if I have this yelling in my head forever? I must be schizophrenic!* Running out of alternatives, I decided I had to face it.

I swear I was sweating, turning green then a pale white. I asked the voice a question in my mind: "If I tell her that you love her, will you leave me alone?"

"Yes. I'll leave you alone if you just tell her. She has to know!"

At that moment, my mother looked over at me and noticed something wasn't right. After all those years of dealing with my panic and anxiety, she knew me well. She asked if I was okay, and I think I mumbled something to her in response, but I couldn't focus on her right now. I had to get this dead person out of my head.

I interrupted Jade's conversation with someone to blurt out, "Jade, will you let me give you a card reading?" I didn't look at my mother to see if she was shocked or not, because I could only handle one calamity at a time, and I was still dealing with my own. Jade had heard about the readings I was doing for friends and anyone else I could talk into it, and she'd been hoping to have one. She smiled but before she could even say a word in response, I had her by the hand and was pulling her over to the kitchen table. I asked her to shuffle the cards, and as she did so I couldn't hold back the message any longer.

"I know this is going to sound crazy, but when you started talking about your father, I felt like I heard him. He wants me to tell you that he loves you. He was adamant that I tell you right away." Even as I said it, I was thinking how crazy I must have sounded. What a lame message—anyone could make that up! So I was almost shocked when I saw the tears begin to pour down her face. She dropped the deck of cards as though *she* was the one who had seen a ghost.

After a long silence, she said quietly, "I'm thirty-five years old, and the one wish I've had my whole life was for my dad to have told me he loved me. He never did. That's all I ever wanted from him."

Okay, so maybe the message wasn't so lame, after all! Still, I was terrified by the whole experience. I was shaking and I needed out of that room. My mom just stared at me in awe, unsure of how I'd just done what I did, but I was far from awestruck. I was completely undone. *Dead people were now in my head,* I thought to myself. *What in the world have I done?*

My best friend, Sandra, had been so supportive of me on this journey. I could tell by the expression on her face that she knew that I was now living my truth. She was the one person who understood, but that didn't seem to help at that exact moment. I looked at her like a deer caught in the headlights, and she smiled back proudly.

When my mom and I got into the car, my mom was the one who was suddenly nervous as she spoke, "Carm, is there something you need to tell me?"

Uh oh. Here it was. Now I had to explain to my mom what had just happened, when I hardly understood it myself. I went into a long explanation, trying my best to make sense of it all, the whole time hoping she wouldn't disown me for good.

"Well, Carmel, that makes perfect sense to me. Your great-grandmother, Nana, was a tea leaf reader."

My jaw hit the floor. I couldn't believe it. *Why did no one ever tell me this?*

I had always known in my heart that Nana and I had a special connection, but this was yet another shocking revelation in a pretty mixed-up day. I was still incredibly confused about everything that had just happened to me. I wasn't sure anymore that this was the path I wanted to take. I wanted to back out of this new bizarre world and go back to my old one, the one where I was just a little crazy. "Crazy" had nothing on this.

Requesting Confirmation from Spirit

The day my mom left to go back home, I sat outside and meditated. I was still confused and desperate for answers. After sitting silently for some time, I called out for help. I didn't search the phone book for a counselor this time. Instead I asked for help from the Other Side, appealing to the only person I felt had any idea what I was going through.

"Nana, if this is true, if this is true about life, if this is true about me, if this is true about God, if this is truly, truly true, then send me back the red jewelry box, and I will believe." I whispered my words into the crisp morning air and let it all go. I felt a sense of calm. By this time I was exhausted from worrying about it all, and I needed to take a break. I went back about the business of my life.

Three days later, my head finally clearer and the request to Nana forgotten, I found myself outside one of my favorite thrift shops. Instinctively, I walked in and grabbed a cart. Grandma always said it was bad luck to shop without a cart, because you'd be sure not to find anything you like!

I casually began browsing through the front aisles where they kept all the antiques. As I walked around the front shelves, where all the good stuff always was, I could feel this man behind me. He was getting closer and closer and starting to make me feel incredibly uncomfortable. I held on to my purse tightly, and he got so close to me, I felt like maybe I should leave. I thought maybe he was trying to steal my bag.

I wasn't quite sure what to do, and I couldn't seem to figure out why he was being so strange, coming so close to me. I decided to go to the back of the store to see if he'd follow me; if he did so, then I could alert the staff. Once I reached the back of the store, he was nowhere to be seen. I was curious; I'd never been to the back of that store before because there was just old Tupperware and kitchen things back there, and I didn't need anything like that. Since I was there anyway, I decided to look around and give the strange man time to leave.

I headed cautiously down one aisle past piles of Tupperware and knickknacks, when out of nowhere I heard a voice that sent chills down my spine. This was not the voice of a creepy man but rather another voice, clearly telling me: "This is the day you will find your nana's box." This voice sounded just like my grandma, so now I was well and thoroughly confused.

"Yeah, right . . ." I said to myself skeptically, but I hadn't even finished the thought when I looked up and saw a flash of gold from a top shelf. I was sure my eyes were playing tricks on me, but there it was—a golden tin leg and a tinge of red. I shook my head, then looked back. It was still there. Could it be? As I took hold of the box and pulled it down, I knew instantly: *It was my nana's jewelry box.*

To my surprise, it was exactly the same as it was the day I left it behind—the day I got on the Greyhound bus back to Edmonton and learned as a young woman to create my own chaos. As I slowly walked toward the front counter, my hands shook. I pushed the cart with one hand and clutched the box tightly with my other. *Was it really Nana's box?* I wondered.

"Of course it's the box, you twit!" my grandma's voice cried out. She had so often used the word *twit,* and while normally it made me laugh, this time her words brought forth tears of joy.

Following in Nana's Footsteps

This is what I'd asked for. She had brought me back the box. I was a medium. I am a medium. This is it. This is what I was meant to do.

I sat in my truck with the box in my lap in total disbelief, just crying and crying. This really happened! *How, Nana? How could you have made this happen?* I suddenly thought about the man at the front of the store. I hadn't seen him again since walking to the back of the store to see if he'd follow. Was he an Angel? Someone my nana sent to help get me to the back of the store where I would never usually go?

That day was a life changer for me, and one I will never forget. *I am a medium.* Even if I wasn't quite ready to tell the world that yet, at least I could proudly say it to myself. I could no longer deny it. I couldn't hide it, or cover it in lies, so I finally decided to embrace it.

Following in the footsteps of my great-grandmother, I began to give readings to friends and family. I gave mediumship readings and also psychic readings if that was what the client wanted or what the Spirits decided. I took a class on being a medium from another local medium, and shortly after that, I decided to start giving my own psychic development class with some other interested friends and like-minded people.

As my abilities grew, so did my client list. Soon those friends were telling other friends who also wanted readings. I printed off some business cards on my computer and let word of mouth do its job. And it wasn't just my clients who were thrilled and amazed. I also came out of each reading on a high, filled with my own amazement that I had known what I had known, unsure how the words were even coming out of my mouth. I would just begin with a card reading and then when the Spirits arrived, I would let the messages flow.

Learning Through The Readings

"What's an intuitive guide?" the young woman asked. One of my business cards had fallen out of my wallet, and she noted the words as she'd picked it up and handed it to me.

"Well, I use cards and intuition to guide people," I responded. I had learned this was a safe answer and sounded the most normal and sane to me. Even though I had taken a class on mediumship, I was still not fully comfortable calling myself a psychic or a medium. I still went into each reading not exactly sure what would happen.

Later, that same young woman brought her friends for a reading. I started with a nicely dressed young woman who looked like she had come straight from church—very conservative looking and incredibly polite. The two of us sat in private while her friends waited their turns in another room. Shuffling the cards as I explained what I did, I accidentally dropped one. As I bent down to pick it up I said, "I crack . . ."

Those were not the words I intended. "I can" was what I'd wanted to say, but for some reason that wasn't what came out. When I looked up at her, I knew instantly why.

"You are a crack cocaine addict," I said, not even considering what the ramifications would be if I were wrong. Embarrassed, she begged me not to tell anyone, because not even her good friends waiting their turns in the living room knew this about her.

I finished her reading and felt that I had been able to offer her some guidance through Spirit, but I had a similar feeling at the end as I did after Jade's father came through. It was a *lack of control.* I had time to adjust to the voices interrupting my thoughts at their will, but this was the first time my actual speech had been interrupted; my words had been changed from *can* to *crack,* and I could not control it.

I was terrified, and deep down I felt that I might still be denying something more. But every time I looked at the gold and red box my nana sent, and every time I looked at my family, I knew denial was no longer any kind of answer, so I kept proceeding with my own healing process and my own learning path.

Sure enough, with each new client, it seemed there was a new lesson for me. All along what I was looking for was my authentic self, and I was getting there with the help of Spirit, one message at a time. The more I helped others, the more I could feel myself healing as well.

For a while it seemed that every client who would find me had gone through something that I, too, had experienced. I was seeing battered woman after battered woman, and so many clients who were hiding shame, who had broken away from their families, who were afraid of being their authentic self. But mostly, I was seeing clients who had not yet forgiven their past, who were still living their life full of guilt, and struggling to find a way to forgiveness, which was the all-important message I discovered when I first read *You Can Heal Your Life*. I began asking for help from my Guides and Angels every day; it's something I still do to this day. It's a practice anyone can and should do, because it is so healing.

Letters from the Heart

As I continued to work on myself, I realized that it wasn't just me who needed to go on this healing journey. I sat down at my desk and picked up my pen, and I asked my Guides and Angels for the courage to put all my truth onto paper, so I could share it with my children.

That day at my desk, I got the help and courage I asked for. I started writing a letter to each of my four eldest children telling them how proud I was of them and how much I loved them. I said the things that mothers should tell their children all the time, but don't always say often enough when life gets going. That's not *why* I was writing, though. I was writing because I had never explained to them my journey. Although they were with me every step of the way, the real journey for me had taken place inside myself—my own unique healing journey. And since it was internal, my kids never saw the utter chaos or the profound changes that I was experiencing deep within.

In my letters to them, I said sorry for every time I ever spanked them, sorry for every parent–teacher interview I never went to, sorry if I didn't hug them enough, sorry that we moved so many times, and sorry for putting men and relationships before them. The kids never heard the voices or felt the fear, the panic, or the shame. They only saw my actions, which were pretty horrific at times. I was worried they might never understand. But now it was time to explain to them why I made the choices I did, and more importantly, it was time that I took *responsibility* for those choices. I was no longer a victim, and I wanted my children to know it.

I was long overdue in clearing the air. Melissa was then 18, Wayne 17, Jessica 16, and Emily 15, and they had learned something most teenagers do as teens: how to guilt-trip their parents. They had begun to use their past, their many moves, their many dads, and their absent mom as fuel to win their arguments with me or to get what they wanted. They were creative and resourceful when they wanted to make their point and get their way.

"Really, Mom? You made us live with Paul for so many years, and you don't understand why I *need* to have a boyfriend?"

"Come on, Mom! You owe us this, after dragging us all the way to Japan and back!"

Yes, they were smart kids, I'll give them that much, but it was time they knew the truth. They knew exactly how to manipulate me because they knew I was still feeling guilty about everything that had happened, particularly about how the choices I had made affected them. For so many years, I had been parenting out of guilt, which was just the same way I was living at the time.

But as I sat down and wrote those letters, something changed. My goal was to help the kids understand why I made the choices I made in life, but what I ended up doing was far more profound. As I wrote, I realized myself *why* I made those choices, and for the first time in my life, *I forgave myself.* At the end of each letter I wrote to them: "I hope that you can find it in your hearts to forgive me, but please know even if you can't, I forgive myself."

As I read each of the kids their letters, one by one, I saw the light bulb flicker on in their heads when I uttered those last words. I could see tears well up in their eyes, and I knew I was giving them what they had needed for years. They needed this whole time for me, as their mother, to be accountable to them for the choices I had made. There was something more, too. You can call it an "aha" moment as they realized that their guilt-trip strategy would no longer work. You can't guilt someone who forgives themselves for their mistakes.

Forgiving myself was an essential step in loving myself. I had to forgive *me* in order to love *me*. After I figured that out—how to love myself—I learned to accept what had happened to me and what I did to my kids and myself. I might have taken away my kids' secret weapon with those letters, but without it, they might not have found forgiveness either. They, too, needed to heal. Without that forgiveness, none of us would have been able to continue on the healing journeys that we were now on together.

And because of that, when Jessica told me some time later that she was pregnant at 17, my reaction was strangely different than with Melissa's news. I knew now that this was her journey. I worried the same way any mother would worry about her daughter, but I embraced it and took the journey with her. I knew now that Jessica had chosen her own lessons to learn in this life, the same way I had, and it was my duty as her mother to respect that. I had given her all of the tools and all of the knowledge she needed, just like Melissa, but somehow life had other plans. There had to be a reason.

Finding Authentic Guidance for Myself

As I began to change, my readings did, too. When I first started giving card readings, mostly intuitive thoughts would enter my head. It felt like the knowledge had come from within me or from just behind me. But more and more often, I found that something different was happening. Messages seemed to come from around my client and outside of me, and not just as thoughts, but as visions, smells, and feelings, too. This was mediumship, and I began to truly embrace this gift; I'd had it all my life but I just didn't know how to use it.

I wasn't quite sure how to react though, and it was hard to find a teacher who wanted to help me. I got rather mixed-up kinds of feedback from the various people I tried to learn from. One of them told me not to do mediumship while I was in their class because I might make the other students feel bad. The Irish healer I went back to told me we weren't all mediums and healers, and that I was getting way too far ahead of myself. Who was I to try to be a healer so quickly when she had spent decades getting to her advanced level of expertise? She insisted that I couldn't just wake up and suddenly have all that knowledge! I began losing hope again. No one wanted to help me or advise me as to what direction to take next.

As I became more frustrated and my confidence started to wane, I prayed every day for someone who knew more about this to help me. I was feeling the same as everyone who was coming to me—lost and needing to know what direction to go. But when everyone was coming to me for that wisdom, who could I turn to myself? There was only one person I could think of—the only psychic I had ever really admired—the one who wrote one of the books that had guided me this far: Sonia Choquette. I looked her up online, booked myself a phone reading, and counted the days and hours until it would happen.

A Reading Just for Me!

"Hi, Carmel," Sonia said when I called the day of my appointment. I was sitting in my car in a parking lot on my cell phone, so Dave wouldn't think I was crazy: one psychic calling another psychic. Even I wondered what would happen. But within a few minutes we were right into the reading, and I was beyond thrilled.

Sonia was eerily right on target about my life. She told me that I had broken away from my family at a young age in order to be able to stand on my own two feet. She knew that I had endured a lot of pain and hardships but that was in order to get me where I was today. She said that very soon it would all become clear to me, too. She said that I would be healing others because of my life experiences and my natural abilities to connect with the Other Side. *Me?* I thought, shocked.

You're probably saying, "Duh! But you've already said you've been doing that." Well, yes, I *was* doing it, but I still had so much inner doubt about my own abilities, and doubt in myself. I'd barely begun to absorb this information when she said something even more shocking.

"Carmel, you are going to help heal the world. You will teach the teachers and heal the healers. You will be world famous! Many people from all over the world will come to you, and you will bridge a gap that will fill the hearts of so many people."

How could I even begin to absorb that? I sat there for a moment, unable to speak, unsure what to say, in shock, but Sonia just kept going. She gave me advice on how to continue developing my gifts, reminding me to meditate and trust what messages the Spirits gave me. She told me I should teach others, and be confident in who I was. It was my "birthright," she said. It was my true authentic self shining through. Sonia told me to ignore what others thought and trust that it was their ego and jealousy that might want to hold me back. As long as I believed in myself, that would be all that mattered.

Curious for advice on some decisions I was too scared to make on my own, I asked Sonia if I should teach a class I was thinking about setting up at the local metaphysical store. "Yes, yes!" she said with bundles of excitement. I almost wanted her to say no, though. I really wasn't sure I was ready to teach, despite feeling pulled to do it.

"None of that matters," she assured me. "Teach what you have learned, and teach it while it's still fresh in your mind, and then go on and learn more and teach more." It sounded like she was telling me to join a gym class or something as commonplace as that, which made her advice all the more empowering.

She continued, "You might not feel ready, but the world is."

Full Steam Ahead with My Plans and Dreams

When the short but amazing phone call was over, I was reeling! Sonia Choquette had just told me I was going to be famous! *How could that be? Could it truly be?* I drove home as fast as I could, tearing in through the front door, and I ran upstairs to find Dave. I was so excited about the news that I had completely forgotten that I hadn't even told him I was getting a reading. But before I knew it, the words were already spilling out of my mouth: "Sonia Choquette says I'm going to be *famous!*"

Confused, Dave looked at me and said in his calm "Yes, dear" way, "And who's that? You'll be famous doing what?"

I picked up two of her books that happened to be next to the bed and dropped them on his lap. "*That's* who she is!" I said, pointing to her name on the covers, as if that meant it *must* be true. Aren't authors of books *always* right?

"That's nice, dear," Dave said completely unfazed. He didn't understand, and he just thought this was another one of my *crazy* ideas, but I was on top of the world! Spirits, here I come! I no longer let it bother me that the Irish healer might laugh at me to her husband, or when friends rolled their eyes. I knew Sonia was right, the Spirits were right, my nana was right, and I just believed.

I taught the class at the store that Sonia said I should, and not long after that, Melissa started to take part in the psychic development classes I was facilitating. I set up the class as a weekly group of like-minded people who could meet to practice their psychic abilities with each other and learn new things. As I watched Melissa learning, growing, and developing an amazing ability of her own, I realized that she had also been hiding her gift.

Seeing my daughter and this group of friends, neighbors, and willing students all practicing together, average people like you and me, that's when I truly understood and accepted that we are *all* psychics and we are *all* mediums. I was happy that Melissa never had anxiety the way I did. I know now that not everyone does. We all have different levels and types of connections with the Other Side.

Soon I was giving readings to as many clients as wanted to come. I decided to build a website, and I established a women's empowerment group that would help women who wanted to start healing journeys of their own to find their authentic selves. People would come to my home to help develop their own gifts and find their truth the same way I had, with Spirit guiding them. One thing just led to another, and the more that came at me, the more I took on. For the first time in my life I felt amazing. *I felt special.* I felt like I was doing what I was meant to do, operating as my own authentic self. I could hardly wait to see what would happen next.

Chapter Fourteen

RULE-BREAKERS

I took one look at this graceful older woman as she walked up to my house for an early appointment, and I thought, *She must be in her 80s.* All I ever know on my calendar is a client's first name, but I could tell by her age that this client would quite likely have a large number of friends and family members in Spirit. When you think about it, the longer you have lived, the more people you've probably lost, which means the more Spirits you bring in my front door. I always find that elderly clients make for amazing mediumship readings, so I braced myself for a lively appointment.

I welcomed her in and helped her get seated, and as I did for every reading, I walked clockwise around my table to my bookshelf and pressed play with my toe on my CD player to start it. While I always like to play soft music in the background, I never do readings without music when I'm in my home, because I have kids—and kids make noise! I always worry that Mike and Keghan might be too loud during my reading with a client, and the music tends to drown out any outside noises.

Puzzling Out the Truth of Spirit

After beginning the reading with a prayer, I started right away. "I have a gentleman here with me, and I think he is your husband." This male Spirit was showing me a vision of Elvis's hair,

THE TRUTH OF SPIRITS

which I found quite funny. Yes, Spirits have a sense of humor, too. "He says he looks like Elvis," I told her.

"Ohhhh yes, dear." The woman clapped her hands together in delight. "But that's not my husband, that's my lover!"

When her actual husband showed up later, I thought it would be awkward, but it seems I was the only one who thought so. There were no hard feelings on the Other Side, although the "lover" did take a step back out of my sight to let the other talk. But it wasn't her husband the elderly lady was most interested in hearing from. When a young girl appeared to me, I knew why this lady had made the appointment. I saw this Spirit as a small female-shaped light crawling up into the woman's lap.

"Did you lose your daughter?" I asked her, and she nodded pleasantly. Clearly this was who she was waiting for. The size of the light sitting there seemed to be of a young child, perhaps only five or six years old. The girl must have died young, and so chose to appear that way as a Spirit to make this clear to me.

As the girl began to sing and dance around the room, I asked the woman, "Did your daughter like to sing and dance?"

The woman assured me that she did. "In fact she took singing and dancing lessons," she remembered fondly. The little girl kept singing and dancing around my reading room and then asked me if I heard the music she was dancing to.

I asked her mother. "Was there something more, something about the music she would sing?" I was unable to figure out the message the little girl was trying to communicate through me, and the elderly woman seemed as puzzled as I was. "Well she loved all kinds of music, that's all I can think of," she said.

Then the little girl spoke to me again. "I shut the music off, so Mummy can hear you!"

I struggled to understand this point, so I asked my client, "Did she stop playing music for some reason?" She shook her head and we both remained puzzled.

"I shut the music off, so Mummy can hear you!" the girl spoke to me once again, in her proud, childish voice. Surely this was important for some reason?

Every single message a Spirit gives me is always right, it is just my interpretation of what they are showing me or telling me that could be incorrect. During this particular reading, I knew we were missing something, because the little girl kept telling me the message, so I just had to keep trying.

As I gave the woman the exact phrase I kept hearing from the Spirit, something caught the corner of my eye. A black cord sprawled across my reading room floor; my CD player was unplugged. To unplug that cord, a person would have had to pull out the shelf and then unplug it. I realized that my music hadn't been playing this whole time and wondered how I hadn't noticed. I play music in every reading!

I thought back to when I walked into the room. If my CD player had been unplugged when I came in, I would have walked over that black cord to get to my desk and surely I'd have noticed it then. Feel free to cue the dramatic music here as you read. Something very strange was going on.

As I looked up at the woman, I noticed her hearing aids for the first time. They were so small and clear, that you had to be straight on and really looking for them to see them. I must have turned white as a ghost as I asked her, "Did you notice that cord when we came in?"

"No, dear. I didn't, dear," she replied. That's when I realized that her daughter had turned the music off, so that her mother could hear me. The message was so simple, but I was in shock and disbelief in that moment. How could that little girl's Spirit have done this?

The woman smiled from ear to ear. "Oh isn't that nice, dear! Because she knew I wouldn't hear you otherwise with my ears being so bad!" She clapped her hands together once more, celebrating what her daughter had done for her.

I barely kept it together for the remainder of the reading. As soon as that lovely lady left, I hollered for the entire family to come into my reading room. "Which one of you unplugged this? Someone had to have unplugged this!" I demanded an explanation from them, but of course they thought I was nuts. They insisted they hadn't touched it, and in fact I knew they couldn't have really done it because I would have noticed the cord when I came in. Still, surely the alternative was not possible. I didn't want it to be true. It remained a mysterious experience, and I had to chalk it up to the little Spirit.

Playing Charades with Spirits

As I've mentioned, I normally see, hear, feel, sense, or smell Spirits when I look at people. They appear to me in various ways, and I have no control over how a Spirit will appear to me; I just accept that they are there. When I'm with clients, I give them the messages that Spirits give me. Often I see the Spirits the way I saw the People when I was five years old. They look like the outline of a body with an aura of light. If the outline is straight it's a male, and if it has curves it's a female. Seems simple enough, right?

Sometimes I can see faces, and sometimes I can see parts of their body if they want to show me a specific thing about themselves, like the size of their nose, or if they were bald, or if they had a tattoo. Once I had a Spirit show me the calluses on his hands. He was a farmer who wanted to tell his daughter how sorry he was for not spending enough time with her as a child because all he did was work. She realized through that reading, however, that this was how he had expressed his love for her, by working hard to provide a good life for his family.

When I hear them it can be like when new thoughts would interrupt my own thoughts in Mr. Thompson's classroom, or an entirely different voice like when Jade's father told me to tell her he loved her. Smelling a Spirit is usually like smelling a particular scent of cologne or perfume that someone wore, a flower that a Spirit was particularly fond of, or smoke if they were a smoker. Feeling them is an entirely different ballgame—and not exactly pleasant at times. I get a sensation in my body, which can be like a shiver, a blast of cold or heat, or very often the feeling of pain in a particular part of my body. That is how Spirits often communicate to me an illness they may have had or how they passed away.

Once while giving a reading to a young woman, I felt this horrible stabbing pain as if someone had pushed a knife into my stomach. I had no idea what the Spirit was trying to tell me, but he said to me "organ," letting me know that he was pointing out a particular organ. Why he couldn't just say the word "kidney" I still don't know—but when I pointed to where I felt the jab of pain, my client knew instantly what it was because her dad had had kidney problems. Maybe I needed to experience it to know how much pain he was in. The feeling goes away as soon as I get the message. While it's there, I just trust that it isn't my pain, and that it will leave me once the message is understood and delivered. Trust me, being a medium isn't as easy as it may look!

I believe it's all based on energy. I think the Spirit chooses how to present themselves to me based on how much energy they have to do it. For example, it probably takes less energy to have me smell smoke than it does to show me the tattoo you have on your arm that was custom drawn and difficult to interpret. As I started seeing more clients, however, the smells, voices, sights, and sounds were starting to come even before the client would arrive, sometimes even the night before if a Spirit wanted to make absolutely sure I remembered to share a message the next day!

Setting the Ground Rules

In the beginning I would see Spirits in my room and Spirits in my bathroom. No, they weren't perverted—they have no ego or concept of time, so they just don't care where you are when they come to give messages. They don't picture nakedness the way we do because, as you'll remember, our physical bodies are simply vessels for our Spirit while we are here. But yet, since you're still thinking about it, it is freaky! I quickly learned I had to make rules with Spirits, and the day the little girl pulled the plug out on my CD player, I knew I had to be even clearer on those rules.

In the same way I would yell at my kids when they had done something completely out of order, I yelled at Spirits. I lectured them in my head, and I spoke as sternly as one can in one's own head. The rules were: Only in my reading room, and no moving, touching, or unplugging anything. I would convey their messages, but *only* if they followed my rules. And that was that.

You're probably thinking—yes, right, but do they listen? And I can tell you that the answer is yes. It seems that Spirits are a bit more obedient than children; children after all are still learning their lessons, while Spirits are helping us to learn ours. Therefore Spirits follow my rules for the most part. And I, for the most part, follow through with my threat not to pass on their message if they don't. But sometimes—just sometimes—there is an exception.

I bend the rules now and again, because I also know that Spirit knows things that I don't know. So, once in a while, Spirit might just know better than me when I should or shouldn't start my readings. I remember one time when I had offered to give two free phone readings on Valentine's Day, and the night before the readings, *both* of the husbands of the women I chose to read for the next day broke the rules.

"Sit up, soldier! You can't be late!" I heard yelling in my ear and felt my shoulders being shaken to wake me. It was 4 A.M. when I opened my eyes, and there was a man in military uniform standing in front of me. "Get out of bed! You need to make sure you shower, brush your teeth, and get all of your candles lit!" he ordered.

Then an hour later, husband number two showed up with a whistle in my ear! "You need to get up. You can't be late today!" he told me. By this time I was pretty annoyed. I thought, *What is it with everyone thinking I'm going to be late today?* It wasn't until the end of the second reading that day that I realized why they may have been rushing me.

I had just told the widow on the other end of the phone how her husband had died—in a car bomb in Iraq—when out of nowhere, I felt something wrap around my neck and choke me. I had never felt anything like it before. I knew it couldn't be this man I was connecting with, but rather it was something scarier. It was a new Spirit, but not one I had invited into my reading. I quickly forced the energy off my neck and, without saying anything to my client, calmly moved forward. Afterward, though, I couldn't shake that feeling.

Figuring Out the Mystery

I sat and meditated while trying to ask Spirit what caused me to feel that choking sensation. Not long after I sat down, a Spirit showed up, and I knew instantly what the feeling had been about. Three days earlier I had received a call from an 18-year-old girl and her 16-year-old brother, hoping I could help find their missing mother. She had disappeared and they were desperate for help. This isn't the first time I'd been called to assist on a missing person's case, but it felt so personal to me as I listened to those two teenagers beg for answers.

I told the kids about their mom, her personality, a recent fight with her boyfriend, and struggles she was having at work, all of which they confirmed. I had connected with her. And I passed along to them good news—she was still alive! I was connecting to her aura but not her Spirit, which meant she had not passed. But I could feel she was physically suffering, falling in and out of consciousness. I felt as if she was in a shed or a barn, near to them, and was taking pills—but not enough to kill her. I could not get completely specific details so I passed along what I could sense.

"There's a suicide note under the bed," I had told them on the phone, because that was the information that seemed to appear in my head. But when they found the note and showed it to the police, rather than proving that there was urgency to the case— that their mom was in real danger—it changed the investigation completely. The police took this to mean that they were no longer looking for a missing mother, but rather a dead body. "But she's still alive!" I insisted as I tried to get the police to listen. But it seemed the more I pushed my point, the more they resisted.

When I finished my Valentine's Day readings, I had meditated, and was still trying to shake that horrible feeling of being choked. Suddenly I had the sinking feeling that there was nothing more that could be done for those teenagers or their mother. I felt their mother appear in front of me, and I knew this time she was in Spirit. She was now gone, and I knew where she was. I called the daughter and told her she needed to ask a policeman to go down a specific path on their property that I knew ran northeast along the river.

"Don't you two go alone. Get an officer to go," I told them very explicitly. I knew what they would find and didn't want them to have to face that alone. The daughter tried three officers, but not one would agree to check that path, so she took her brother and a friend and off they went. They found their mother's body hanging from a tree.

I felt horrible that the police officers on their mother's case couldn't seem to get past their own egos enough to trust the advice. Being a mother, my concern was for the children who should not have had to find their mother in such a way.

I know that there are police officers who are open to other forms of "investigation," however, and I have gotten quite a few calls from the police and from families to help out with missing-persons cases and unsolved crimes. I do my best now to help when and where I can, as I've learned that Spirit will bring everything to you that you need to be working on.

Setting Rules for Myself

As I have developed this as my career path, I set rules for myself as well, not just for the Spirits. After Dave's reading went so badly, I made a rule that I would not do readings for my children until they were at least 18 years old. I felt like they needed to be adults to understand the messages and to respect the guidance they were being given.

But who said rules weren't for breaking? Well, at least that's what the kids had figured, and two of them managed to somehow convince me to be a bit flexible on that "rule." Keghan was the first to get a reading. He has always been the persuader. He came to me one day after a client left and looked up at me with those big brown eyes no one can deny. "What is a medium, Mom?" he asked, knowing full well what it was but wanting me to explain anyway. I figured since he occasionally handed out my business card at school if one of his teachers asked about me, that I might need to explain more. When I finished telling him some details, he announced, "I need a reading."

I said no at first, but he was so adamant I finally gave in, figuring I'd just fake it. I brought him into my reading room, had him sit down, and thought, *I'll just make up something.* But even if I wanted to make something up, I should have known that the truth would make its way through. Our imagination, after all, is the easiest way for Spirits to communicate with us, and there is no ego there.

Sure enough, just as I sat down, I felt a sudden sadness come over me. Keghan was so sad that I didn't even need to start using my imagination to feel what he was feeling. "You miss Tucker, Bud," I realized, saying it out loud. Tucker was a beautiful yellow Labrador puppy we adopted when we were in Japan, and he'd become Keghan's best friend. Even though my son was only about three at the time, he still thought of him. What he remembered most clearly, though, was the day he saw Tucker get hit by a car, a day that still saddened him five years later.

"Keggie, you still have an immense amount of guilt over what happened to Tucker," I said to him, and his eyes began to fill with tears. Keghan had opened the door to let our other dog, Pepper, out when Tucker had pushed past him. He'd never meant to let Tucker out, but he was so small he had no way of stopping the dog as he ran across the street after the female dog of the neighbors. Tucker darted in front of a truck, which could never have stopped in time. It all happened right in front of Keghan's eyes, and he never forgot it.

I passed along the message from Spirit that Keghan needed to hear: "Keg, Tucker is right here with you. He is with you all the time, you don't have to carry this burden. You can let this go."

"That's why I was asking for a dog, Mom," Keghan explained. "I feel like if I get a new yellow Lab, that Tucker will reincarnate into the one I choose."

I knew Dave was against getting another dog because we had just put down our Great Dane and we hadn't quite healed yet. But as I watched Keghan pour his heart out over Tucker, I wanted nothing more than to heal his wounds. Dave still wasn't convinced when I told him I thought we should get a new dog for Keghan, but armed with the knowledge from my reading, I finally convinced him it was a good idea.

I don't know how Keghan knew it would all turn out, but this little puppy was just as fanatical about Keghan as Tucker had been. He named the pup Tucker's Little Buddy (Buddy, for short). Wherever Keghan went, Buddy was never far behind. The dog would even jump out of the window and get stuck on the roof if Keghan left the house and didn't take Buddy with him!

A few months later, when we moved to a new acreage, someone came onto our property and stole Buddy along with another dog, Maddy. We don't know who, or why, but it tore my heart out to see Keghan have to grieve all over again. We spent months looking for Buddy and Maddy. We searched the river valley behind our house for weeks, and never found even a clue.

After realizing we might never find them, we decided to hold an event to raise awareness in the area about "dog-nappings" and missing pets. We called it "Missing Mutts Awareness," and our first event had about 750 people show up. We were so thrilled to have 7 dogs from the local rescue organization adopted into loving homes that day, and 32 dogs received microchip trackers. We have now turned it into an annual event.

Perhaps Keghan had to go through that pain to help other dogs; or maybe it wasn't my place to heal him. I think this was a lesson that was his alone, and I could not be the one to learn it for him, even though my heart broke to see him suffer these losses. We all have our own life lessons and no one can take them from us, even if they try.

Spirit Always Tells the Truth

Keghan was not the only one to sneak a reading out of me before turning 18. Emily was only 17 when she demanded one, too. I went ahead because I wondered if giving her a reading early would help with some recent arguments she was having with her boyfriend. Maybe I could show her there would be a light at the end of the tunnel. I mean, how much could there be to tell a 17-year-old? Apparently, quite a lot.

The first few cards I flipped told us more than either of us had bargained for. "You're going to get pregnant!" I blurted out, unable to stop the message.

Emily was appalled and said, "Mom, I can't believe you would say that!"

I couldn't believe I'd said it either, but there's no lying when you're speaking for Spirit. Emily had been with her boyfriend for nearly three years, and she was adamant that they were far too careful to accidentally get pregnant.

"No, you're going to break up—and you're going to be hurt and angry. You'll go out to a party and have too much to drink, and you'll have a one-night stand, and you'll get pregnant." It was almost as if I wasn't speaking to my own daughter. Surely this isn't something you should be telling your daughter. This was nothing like Emily's character, and something I myself couldn't even believe would happen. But the cards just aren't wrong, and I knew that.

"Mom," Emily said again, horrified. Then she stormed out.

That was that, I said to myself. No more reading the kids!

Three months later, however, Melissa got a call as the two of us were standing in the aisle at the grocery store. I knew instantly who was on the phone and what the news was. "Answer the phone, your sister is pregnant," I said. Melissa looked at me in shock, then was even more surprised to find Emily in tears on the other end of the phone, blubbering out that she was pregnant.

The truth was, I was worried for her, my young daughter. Terribly worried because I knew what I had had to endure as a teenage mother. But what I also knew was that this was not something I could change. I'd given Emily fair warning; both Jessica and Emily should have learned from Melissa. Emily had not only her sisters' example but a pretty specific warning from Spirit, yet life had other plans.

I'm not an advocate for teen pregnancies, but at the same time, I know that parents can only do so much. You can lead a horse to water, but you can't make it drink. I know I had given my kids all the tools they needed to prevent it, but regardless we now have three beautiful grandchildren. And as it turns out, if they hadn't gotten pregnant when they did, perhaps we never would have had any grandchildren. All three of them later found out that they had certain complications that would make having a baby, even just conceiving, nearly impossible. Somehow they were blessed and are fulfilling their divine truth as young mothers at this time, and continuing to discover their true life paths along the way.

My unconditional love for them and for all members of my family is a big part of my own path and my own journey. I embraced unconditional love wholeheartedly, once I had learned to truly love myself *unconditionally*. That key was tremendously important to my growth, and I thought it was the hardest thing to master. But then with all these family circumstances and the property and the animals and my new career path as a medium and public presenter—that all came with its own big challenge, the last of the four keys I had to learn to master: *balance*.

I've come a long way, but I still sometimes get caught up on that one.

Chapter Fifteen

REIGNITING THE FLAME

In my second year into giving readings to clients, I was preparing for my 40th birthday—or so I thought. Turns out I was actually turning 39; what a bonus! Somehow, I'd gone years thinking I was one year older than I'd really been. I felt that this called for a real big celebration! A month before the big day, Dave surprised me with an early birthday present: horseback-riding lessons.

I had been on the fence about whether or not I should try horseback riding again, and when I found out I was a whole year younger than I thought, I figured, you only live once (or twice that year, in my case). So I decided I wanted to overcome my fear of horses. During my childhood, watching my father's horses react in fear to his booming voice and terrible temper, I developed a fear of horses myself. But since I had learned to forgive my father, I thought I should also learn to forgive horses.

Dave didn't know quite what to think when I first requested lessons, but after having the neighbor's horses on our property for a few days, Dave quickly fell in love with their beauty. He spent days gazing out the window with me at the majestic beasts as they mowed down our overgrown lawn. I could tell that they had sparked an interest in him, and I instantly knew it wouldn't be very hard to convince him I wanted to ride.

I asked Dave to help me conquer my fear of them. He'd seen me grow and heal myself of so many other deep-seated fears and become a whole new person. However, after that first reading, which was nearly two years ago at this point, we hadn't really talked much about what I was doing with my psychic abilities.

Seeking a Point of Reconnection

While I'd gone off on my healing journey these past months, Dave went on his own journey. We still had our family and our lives together that kept us connected, physically. We still discussed work, friends, and the funny things the kids did or how the dogs probably needed another four-legged friend to play with. Emotionally, however, we were becoming more and more disconnected.

Perhaps that's why my husband surprised me by giving me an incredible horse to go along with the riding lessons. It didn't take long for me to fall in love with that horse, and it brought out a new dimension between Dave and me—a new interest for us that we could experience together. Better yet, this was an interest Dave could wrap his head around, and it was amazing how fast it rekindled our personal connection. When Dave purchased another horse, he and I found a new common ground. At first, he didn't know that much about these majestic animals we had begun to take such a keen interest in, but he was just as intrigued as I was to learn more.

As we began to spend time together again, Dave began to unplug from unhealthy friendships, and plug into a newfound peace and calmness that the horses brought out in us both. Dave would spend as many hours as he could building fences and gates for the horses, and even turned his beloved bike garage into a barn. Some of his biker friends didn't think that was cool. Instead of paying off a loan on a new bike, we were buying saddles and boots. It was hard not to dive into something that brought us so close and gave us so much joy and peace.

Soon the kids were riding horses as well, and what surprised us all was Mike's newfound love for horseback riding. Still recovering from her stroke and struggling to regain the use of her hands and fingers, she was able to ride horses as if she had been born to do it. Her recovery picked up speed, and before we knew it, she could do anything. She was outriding adults with three times the experience she had, and she was determined to get back full use of her hands.

With the horses now at the center of our family, holding us together, the house and property we had was no longer big enough. We searched and searched for a property we could afford, that would give us more room for the horses but fit within our budget. It was Spirit who found us the place in the end. While Dave and I were in the truck, headed out of town to a horse sale, a voice interrupted my thoughts. It told me my house was awaiting me and to check Kijiji, an online classified ads site where homes are often listed.

I hesitated at first, because I knew how much Dave hated when I was on my phone if we were spending time together. The voice just kept saying, "Check Kijiji, the house you want is there." So eventually I caved, and began to scroll through the rental homes. I was doubtful I would find anything, since I had just checked those listings that morning. Lo and behold, there it was: 43 acres, just on the market, and even cheaper than what we were paying for our current, smaller place! We saw it the next day, and signed the papers before we left.

Within months we were moving away from our first home together, the one we had back when we were a leather-clad biker couple with a blended family. Now we were moving into our new home as one strong family unit, peaceful and hopeful. When we left, some of the friends we'd made while in that previous house, while we were in that old state of being, also moved on from our lives; and new friends emerged.

We all became interested in new things, and we were all becoming new people it seemed; we weren't just acquiring new hobbies but growing spiritually as well. That one desire for horses saved us all, I think, because it gave us such a solid common ground. It also helped us realize the importance of sharing our journeys. It's what Dave calls the importance of *staying the same color.*

Keeping Your Colors in Mind

When Dave and I were once again journeying together, he explained something very important to me that has become our marriage's number one rule: the concept of *colors.* "When you fall in love with someone, you are blue and they are red. Then you become purple, and you *love* purple. But if you start not liking purple, you can change it to green, both of you. If one of you decides they like a different color, the two of you have to share it so you can stay the same color, even if it's a different shade.

"As a couple then, each person has to make sure they each have that bit of extra color so they can understand why the other is changing, and so the other person doesn't end up still feeling like they are purple when their spouse has become bright yellow."

I'm glad Dave found a way to explain this to me, and I have since explained it to other people. It is a great way to keep your intimate connection to your spouse. I saw what happened first-hand when I ignored our relationship and changed "color" suddenly with no thought for the consequences. When I dove headfirst into the world of Spirit, I didn't just forget to take Dave with me, I didn't even tell him where I was going! I changed "color" drastically, and he didn't know why—and it nearly tore us apart.

I believe it probably would have broken our connection, if it weren't for the horses. Dave and I rarely ride anymore because we both have back issues. Nonetheless, they have become an incredible shared passion and an integral part of our family life, especially the kids' lives. The horses, in my opinion, have been Mike's saving grace as well. Looking back, I think that Spirit was pushing the horses into our lives to save our marriage, to save Mike, and to change the direction of our lives for the best. The same way Spirit helped us find our current home—the home we still live and love in today!

In the process of the move and my yearning to connect with Dave again, I had pulled away from the world of Spirit. I felt that my giving readings had pushed Dave and me apart, so I stopped doing them. It started with not having time to fit as many clients in, once my schedule was filled with horse lessons. But before long, I found that I wasn't giving any readings at all.

Before the horses had arrived, my client roster had grown so large that I found myself giving readings all hours of the day and night. I read for anyone and everyone who asked for a reading, and I would give and give to no end. I poured my heart and soul into each and every reading, and it was draining me—emotionally, physically, and spiritually. I was, quite literally, *spent.*

Returning to My Own Lesson Plan

Often people watch mediums give readings and think that they are merely talking. "What a gift. How incredible and effortless it looks," they say. "Especially for people who like to talk!" And, yes, I do like to talk! But people don't see how much energy is behind it all. I can assure you that giving a reading requires much more physical, emotional, and mental energy than most people would think.

In every reading, my heart is beating wildly, almost out of control, my palms are sweating, the room is sometimes spinning, and I'm often receiving physical sensations to go along with all of that. It can be very much like having a panic attack, except I'm not scared anymore. I now know what it is, and I have learned to feel safe because I know these feelings are not my own.

The hardest part of being a medium, however, is honoring that it takes an enormous amount of work to connect with the Other Side. Often mediums end up overworking as they try to help as many people as they can. They forget to respect the process, the energy, the vessel. In this case, I am referring to our physical bodies, our minds, and our own divine Spirit, which I have come to learn must be put first. In every reading, a medium must ramp up their own energy to be able to communicate with a deceased person who is now in another realm. That's not easy.

In my case, I was exhausted because I had given and given, so much so that my well was dry. Then, as the icing on the cake, I allowed myself to *feel guilty* for feeling like it was "work." I wanted it to be easy and Spiritual and seamless like it seemed to be on TV and in all the books. I learned later that other mediums and healers don't really discuss that side of it, how draining it can be.

Once I started feeling guilty about this work, I felt like it triggered very unpleasant reminders of all that guilt I had just overcome from my past. I no longer wanted any guilt or shame in my life. I was so exhausted and depleted that I felt I had no choice but to let go and stop doing any of the psychic or healing work. I had to stop because I was no longer teaching what I was preaching: I was advising all my clients to love themselves, but I wasn't loving myself.

Reviving My Energy Through Pure Love

I imagine that many readers of this book have been in a similar place, where you felt that you just couldn't do *something* anymore, like you were drowning with no land in sight. If someone asked for one more favor, if you heard one more "Please, Mom," if you got just one more request from a friend or colleague, then you might just topple over and never get back up. Or, at least, never *want* to get up because you didn't have the energy!

I was terrified of losing myself again, so I withdrew. But then I wondered what would happen if I was no longer able to live my truth. *So much for being famous,* I thought, looking at Sonia Choquette's book on my bedside table. Maybe all this just wasn't for me. I stopped taking calls from clients, I pulled the plug on that life I had been living, and I dove into the horses full-time. Oh, Carmel—still the all-or-nothing girl.

I took several horse-riding lessons a week with the kids and tried to put my life of readings out of mind, but an amazing thing happened. The connection I built with my horse, and the relationship it started rebuilding with Dave and my family, started to revive me. My horse became my lifeline. He slowly and surely replaced every ounce of energy that I had given to others, and he gave back to me unconditionally and completely.

I look back at it now and think that maybe it was in the plans the whole time. Maybe that horse was always supposed to save me, the way a horse saved Mike and brought her back to health, and the way he breathed new life into my relationship with Dave. But when I dug deeper, there was still more to it. By focusing on the horse, I was focusing on me. I was putting my needs first, my need to be my authentic self. Being with the horses had become my meditation, a practice that I had been giving less and less time to, because I kept choosing to put the needs of my clients above my own personal needs.

I found out that meditation doesn't mean you have to sit on the ground, cross your legs as uncomfortably as you can, and be still for hours on end. Living in the now, being present in the moment, that is also a powerful form of meditation—and for me, once I spent time with my horse, I was finally being present.

Returning to Mediumship

Once I felt healed and whole, my life path took shape once more. It was just a normal day (I know you've heard me say that before), when things changed again. Just a few months after I stopped giving readings, I was out at the barn feeding the horses when my cell phone rang.

"Carmel, you have to come back!" It was one of my old clients on the other end of the line. I hadn't spoken to a client for months—avoiding calls to avoid the guilt—and I'm not sure what led me to answer this call, but I'm glad I did.

She continued, impassioned: "Your gift changed my life and the lives of so many of the people I know. Every friend and loved one I have sent to you is now a changed person, a healed person. This is what you are meant to do. Please don't walk away from

Spirit. Don't let go of this ability you have to help heal the world." It was almost as if an Angel had come to Earth to tell me to get back on my true path and do what I was meant to do.

After our call, I took a deep breath and sat down on the bench outside the barn. I knew she was right. I knew what I had been doing helped so many people, but at the same time I knew I had to find a healthy balance between Spirits, my family, and myself. When I was doing readings, my children never saw me, and my husband was unsure of exactly what I was doing; all I wanted was to make all the parts of my life fit and coexist together as one.

I truly wanted to live my life's purpose, and I knew what that was. But I didn't want my marriage to the man I loved or my relationships with my children to suffer because of it. I had learned so many life lessons throughout my journey, but the journey never ends. This time Spirit was teaching me about balance. Confused and unsure of what to do after that call, I knew just who to ask for help. I went back to my nana. I knew she would give me the right guidance.

"If this is really what I am meant to do, please send me a blue butterfly," I said as I sat in our barn in the middle of winter. I have no idea why I chose a blue butterfly. I liked them and thought they were pretty, and hey, that's a good enough reason for me when I'm shopping, so why not use that now?

I got back up and headed into the barn because I could now hear Dave in one of the stalls cleaning up without me. I started talking to him about the phone call from the client, and I sat down on a chair outside the stall he was working in. What happened next still feels like a dream to me.

One single butterfly came fluttering down from the roof of the barn and landed on my knee. On December 21st, in the middle of a bitterly cold winter, a beautiful blue butterfly landed on my knee. The barn is heated, but *really?* If that's not a sign, I don't know what is. (Yes, okay, the jewelry box was a pretty impressive sign, too.)

As I watched the butterfly flutter out the barn door, with snow falling down just outside, I knew what I had to do. I also knew that my nana would be with me to support me every step of the way.

Balancing My Work with Everything Else

When I started doing readings again this time, I decided I needed to find my balance. I needed to be a wife and a mother just as badly as I needed to be a healer. Here's the thing about finding your authentic self—it can't just be part you; it's an all-or-nothing game. I'm an all-or-nothing girl as I have said, so you'd think I'd be perfect at this.

But what I had been missing in my life up to this point was the understanding that in order to have it all, I would have to have it all *in moderation.* It's all about balance, and with balance comes the ultimate lessons in self-love. Yes, back to that all-important concept that underlies everything—*self-love.*

This time, before I returned to my clients, I hired an assistant. In fact, Spirit hired me an assistant, sending me the perfect person at just the right time! A woman who came to my classes before we moved was eager to take the position, and I was grateful to have the help. I had so much faith in my gift now that my energy was renewed. I just knew the clients would come and I would need someone to help me keep the appointments and the business side of it in balance.

I believe that if you do what you love and love what you do, life will begin to change around you; and that's exactly what happened. Soon I was back to having nonstop calls for readings, but this time I had some help to set healthy boundaries for how much work I would take on. I saw clients during business hours only; although I sometimes made exceptions, I always put me and my family *first.*

The critical balance I'd been missing had been found, and not only did my family benefit but my clients did as well. Spirits seemed louder and my ability to connect became easier because I was rested and physically well. By this time, we had ground rules in place for everyone—not that everyone always followed them, but at least the rules were there!

Dave probably appreciated this new approach more than anyone. It was bad enough that he didn't really know what was happening in my reading room when clients were around, but having me wake up at 2 A.M. speaking to invisible people probably didn't help. I had taken the time to explain to Dave what I was doing and what I saw and felt, but because my readings were private, he had never seen them happen—except of course for our little experience with my oracle cards. But that hadn't involved any loved ones coming through from the dead to speak to him.

Understanding "Energy" at Work

When I described my work to Dave, I decided to start by explaining "energy." It was a concept I thought he could relate to. Everything is made of energy; you're energy and I'm energy, it's something we all already know. This book is energy and the seat you're sitting on is energy. Energy with a physical body moves quite slowly because it has so much mass to lug around. Energy without a physical body moves more quickly—fast as lightning.

Think about it: electricity has no physical bounds to it so it moves faster than we can see or imagine. The only thing Spirits have lost is their physical body. So a Spirit's energy is moving very, very quickly. When they come around and get up close to us, we pick up on that energy. This sensation is what caused me to feel such anxiety and suffer with panic attacks for so many years.

I believe Heaven is just outside our aura, and our loved ones are with us all the time. When I'm not giving readings, I can feel all that energy build up around me. They know I can hear them, feel them, see them, and smell them, so they come in close. Sometimes they're relentless in their efforts to get me to pay attention. Reading for clients is a way to release that energy and do what I was meant to do, but it's also what the Spirits need for me to do. It's work and some Spirits are easier to connect with than others. I do my best to give every single client an amazing connection with the Other Side.

Dave never felt what I felt, nor did he read the books I read, and as much as he wanted to understand my energy analogy, let's face it—it can sound a bit kooky! When Dave would have the odd encounter with a client as they left a reading, they would tell him how amazing I was—how I had healed them or shocked them—but that didn't give him a vision of what had truly just transpired. I tried to share with Dave my new "color" by describing to him all the amazing Spirits that had come through in a reading, or the groundbreaking healing experiences that I had with a client, but telling someone about a reading is like going to Niagara Falls and bringing back pictures. The pictures prove how immense and grand the falls are, but they don't show the "awe effect"—the feeling of nature's raw power that you get by standing in front of it yourself.

Dave would say, "That's nice, honey," when I'd tell him about a reading, the same way he would if I told him about the great dress I found on sale when I was out shopping. That is, until one day when Dave was able to witness my gift for himself, the day our colors truly became one again.

Open Mediumship

Since starting up readings again, I had a desire to be able to help more than just one person at a time. I knew that all great mediums eventually must learn how to give readings to bigger groups, something we call "open mediumship." I had never before attempted to give a reading to more than two or three people. I had spent my whole life avoiding large groups of people, and now I was considering bringing a large group of strangers into my home? The more people, the more Spirits, the bigger the challenge! I was terrified, but still pretty excited at the prospect.

When I look at people, I see their loved ones. Imagine one person who has lost several family members; that one person can bring in several Spirits just on their own. As I've said, it's why I get a bit nervous with older clients! Now consider a whole roomful of people, each with five or six or more Spirits tagging along! I was worried I would lose control over my anxiety and over the Spirits that I had worked so hard to peacefully communicate with. But something was really pushing me to try this—so finally I did.

Dave's voice announced: "It's my pleasure to introduce to you all, my wife . . . here is Carmel Baird." It was the very first open mediumship event we had arranged at our house, and Dave was under strict orders not to tell any jokes or long-winded stories. After he said his one line, I walked into the room and took a big gulp of water before starting. *Here we go.*

It all started with one Spirit. I looked down at a man who had come with his wife to the group. His arms were crossed, and I could tell he was a total skeptic. Sure, why not pick a challenge for my first reading of the night?

"Your dad has passed," I said. He nodded, not very impressed. Okay, so that was how it was going to go. No problem. I knew I had a strong Spirit, and it was going to be an easy connection. The flash of a car emblem prompted me to ask the man about his truck—specifically a Chevy. A shocked look spread across the man's face. I continued to repeat every word and every vision the Spirit gave me after that. He described how he loved to golf with his son and wished they had one more day to do that together. The Spirit told me to tell his son that he was proud of him and knew that he hadn't told him that enough. (That seems to be the most common message Spirits wish to let us know, so make note of it for yourself: Don't wait until it's too late to tell your family members that you love them and you are proud of them.)

Tears were now forming in the man's eyes. His tough exterior seemed to disappear as he heard the words he so desperately needed to hear from his father. Spirit was happy, I was happy. When I asked the man for a hug at the end of that part of the event, he hugged me for both his dad and for himself. I knew then that he was happy, too.

I also knew in that very moment that I could *do* this. I continued down the line from person to person until I was done reading all 20—what a rush! Exhausted, but on a high I'd never before experienced, I finally brought myself back down into the room. I lowered my vibration back to our usual level as I said thank you and good night to this room of strangers I felt so connected to.

As I turned around I saw Dave, who had watched the entire event. He was white as a ghost, mouth open, and tears poured down his cheeks. I knew then that he was now the same "color" as I was, not even a shade darker or lighter. He believed, but more importantly, he *understood.*

I had to love myself before I could fully love Dave. Although I unplugged from Dave, and changed "colors" without telling him, I know now that *had* to happen because I had to learn to love my own new "color" first. It's important that you are the same "color" as your partner, but it's even more important for you to love your own "color." *Yes, self-love.*

◎ ◎

Chapter Sixteen

MOM'S A MEDIUM

When I greeted my client at the door that morning, I could instantly tell that he had no interest whatsoever in being there. I can always tell when a male client has been nagged into coming to see me. "Your wife dragged you here, didn't she?" I said after we'd introduced ourselves. It probably didn't blow him away that I knew that, since it was written all over his face.

"Good one," he said begrudgingly, obviously waiting to be impressed—or more likely to be *unimpressed*. "She thinks I need to come see a healer, or something, so I'm here. Most of this stuff is hokey pokey but I'm here, so let's see what you got."

As much as I like to prove someone wrong, I felt a little daunted. Here was a man in his 70s, sitting across from me with his arms crossed, waiting to get out of my reading room and prove to his wife that this was all just a big waste of his time. He seemed pretty certain of his truth, but I was up for the challenge. He was blunt and cheeky; but then again, I would be, too, if I was in his position. Time for a Spirit intervention!

His father showed up first, and I passed along details about his childhood and how proud his father was of him. Next his mother's Spirit came through to tell me her son was sick recently and how she helped him get through it. Tears began to form in his eyes as this man said, yes, he had recently battled cancer and how he was praying he was in remission. The mother Spirit assured her son he was, indeed, in remission, and the comfort that came to him that morning was something he really needed to hear.

He was winning the battle with his health, and Spirit needed him to know he wasn't alone. His mother's Spirit talked to him through me about his love of music and movies. His parents just kept the messages coming so he would truly feel their support and love as he continued to face the challenge of healing.

You might think that I would be used to seeing people cry by now, but I'll tell you, I never get used to seeing a man in tears in my reading room. We are programmed by society to believe that men should be tough and have it all together so much so that when a man starts to tear up in front of me, I can't pass him the box of tissues quick enough. In fact, we shop at Costco for this in my line of work!

I've learned through giving readings that we all need to feel loved. And as we open ourselves up to receiving that love, it's only natural that we feel vulnerable. I am there to let all my clients know, male or female, young or old, that we are all human and we all feel the same way.

Extending Messages to the Masses

Collecting his thoughts and still a bit pale from the profound messages he had received, the man pulled his chair back a bit, uncrossed his arms, and looked at me.

"You need a TV show. This is for real!" he said.

"Oh yeah, right," I laughed. I was just happy that he wouldn't be telling his wife that it had been a waste of time after all.

"No, really," he continued. "I used to be a producer, and believe me—you need a TV show!"

I just chuckled at the idea as I followed him to the door. I gave him a big hug and smiled as I watched him walk down the path. I continued smiling to myself on the way to the kitchen. *A show on TV. What an idea.*

Then, a few weeks later, as I was driving over the railway tracks on my way home from grocery shopping, I heard Spirit say a single word: "Slice."

"Slice?" I said it out loud to myself in the car. A slice of what? I had no clue what Spirit could be talking about, but I knew I didn't get any messages without a reason. *What the heck is this one about?* I thought. By now I'd gotten used to crazy messages and strange thoughts coming into my mind out of nowhere. However, I always trust Spirit, and I know that everything means something, so I set off to find out.

"What does *slice* mean?" I called to Dave when I got home.

"What do you mean? A slice of what?" he asked.

Oh good, he was as confused as I was. "I don't know! I just heard it. *Slice.* Is it a company?"

Dave thought about it for a moment. "It's a television channel," he said very matter of fact, with really no idea of what was going on. But he was used to this, playing guessing games about words that would come to me from Spirit.

At the time, I hardly ever watched TV and *never* watched the news. Even now, I prefer to stick with my predictable DVDs; with movies, I'm not likely to get a Spirit bomb!

But in this case with Slice, Spirit knew what was coming and was preparing me for the next message I'd receive. Maybe even reminding me how powerful a connection we had built together, Spirit and me.

That afternoon I got an e-mail from Slice TV inquiring about my family and what I did as a medium. They were interested in creating a TV show about me.

Filming Mom's a Medium

"What do you think?" I asked Dave, explaining the reading I'd had a few weeks earlier with the retired producer. He must have been more serious than I thought about his TV idea.

"Well, why not?" Dave said. What could it hurt for us to send them some home movies and our information? We could do that. As if we would ever be chosen anyway. It was still a long shot.

We were still doubting that all this would ever turn into anything when the film crew arrived to film a "sizzle reel." The point of a sizzle reel is to pitch a new concept for a show to the network. In this case, the network had already come to us asking for the pitch! As it turned out, we weren't what Slice wanted or what they were looking for at that time. We knew that might be the end of it and nothing further for the show's development might be pursued, but our production company believed in our family so it didn't stop there.

The network that wanted us in the end was CMT Canada, owned by Corus Entertainment, and before we knew it, we were filming season one of *Mom's a Medium*. That's when my list of job titles officially expanded—from medium, mom, intuitive guide, teacher, and wife—to include one more role on the list: reality-TV star. Not a bad addition, if you ask me!

Well, yes all right, perhaps "star" is a bit of an overly glamorous title. After all, it's *reality TV!* Filming a TV show is a lot more work than one might think. It's a bit like mediumship in that it seems the whole thing takes on a life of its own. We spend our days with a lot of people around us, and you certainly have to get used to the idea of cameras around you all the time. At first, I felt like my life was being lived under a microscope! Cameras follow my entire family; the animals on the ranch; and, if they agreed to be filmed, my friends, workshops, and personal clients—all the different things that make my life tick.

So imagine this: You know how when you're having a dinner party, you make sure that the kids get a good strict talking-to before the guests arrive so they are on their best behavior, and you make sure to clean all those parts of the house that you generally, well, never clean? When the cameras are following your every move, you no longer have that option! Perhaps I'd been in training for this part of my life, having spent all those years keeping up appearances, which were really nothing more than lies and pain. Because it has been surprisingly easy to have cameras follow me and my family around; and to be honest, we've had a great deal of fun doing it!

The kids adjusted well, too, like the troupers they are. Keghan and Mike had always loved it whenever we had a house full of Dave's leather-clad friends over, and this idea of having people with lights and cameras was sort of like that. Living in this happy chaos was second nature to them, complete with antics, pranks, and lots of laughter. Keghan quickly found new basketball buddies with our cameramen, and my grandson Ben keeps everyone in stitches with his funny gestures and jokes.

I learned quite a bit, too. The director, Tara, taught me how to eat a healthier diet. I mean, did you know there are other ways to eat than directly out of plastic containers? Or is that breaking news only to me?

My favorite thing that happened during the filming of season one was when my mentor, Sonia Choquette, came to the ranch. I was so happy that Sonia, the same woman who told me I would be famous, was giving me a reading on my own show. She helped Melissa get back on track with her readings and gave her the push she needed to become more confident in her abilities, in the same way that she'd helped me many years before.

But wait; it gets even better. Sonia told me she felt that my personal story should be heard by the world and connected me with her publisher in California. I could hardly believe it; I now had the chance to publish my story with the company founded by the same woman whose book changed my life, Louise Hay. It was her groundbreaking book that started my whole journey to discovering my authentic self. I feel such gratitude and love for her, because her words were truly the catalyst of my own healing journey and transformation.

Whose Spirits Belong to Whom?

Anyway, when we started to film season one, I never imagined what it would be like to have other people in my reading room with me. No one is filmed without agreeing to it, of course. Still, the first time I sat down to give a reading with a camera over my shoulder and another over my client's shoulder, it was *so* strange.

When I meet with a client one-on-one, the two camera people are the only ones allowed in the room; that was something I was adamant about. My only other rule that I gave the production company was that once a reading starts, nothing stops it. No interruptions whatsoever, because that could risk me losing the connection with the Spirits.

What I didn't plan on was a Spirit coming in that belonged to one of the crew! The first reading we filmed for season one turned out to be a reading for both the client as well as one of the cameramen. I don't think the cameraman was a huge skeptic, but he wasn't a 100 percent believer either. During the reading, a Spirit in the form of an elderly man kept interrupting the messages I was getting from the client's mother. "Is your grandfather passed?" I asked her.

"No," she said.

That's so strange, I kept thinking. *Who could it be?* I was so intent on getting in touch with her Spirits, I didn't even think of the others. After all, I wouldn't normally have two extra people hanging out in my reading room.

This just goes to show that I don't have control over what messages come through. When Spirits wants to talk, it's my job to listen. I actually think I work for the Spirits more so than for the client, since it is the Spirits that hold the reins. Once this grandfather Spirit decided he was going to come through, well, we all just had to go with it.

I gave my client a message about how proud the Spirit was that she had his watch. He talked about seeing a wedding and so much more, but none of it seemed to make any sense to her. "Maybe it's a message for someone you know," I suggested and shrugged it off.

How embarrassing of these Spirits, I thought, *to send me off on such a sideways direction. And on our first day of filming no less!*

Once I got the grandfather figure settled away, the client's mother did come back in and connected in the usual way, with messages that gave the client some proof that it was really her. My favorite message from the mom in this case was that she loved how long her daughter's hair was. She wanted me to let her know how beautiful it looked. The woman laughed and told me she hadn't cut her hair since her mom passed. When she was a young girl, her mom had always cut her hair for her, so this comment on her hair was a reference to the deep bond between them.

Finally the reading was over, and I stood up and hugged the client good-bye. I sighed, relieved that we had survived our first filmed session. Then I saw that one of my cameramen was white as a ghost. "Umm, Carmel," he said, tears filling his eyes. "That was my grandfather. All those messages were for me. I have my grandpa's pocket watch, and all those things you said about him are true. I can't believe it. *This is real.*"

Touchdown for me! Two new believers in one day!

Lasting Effects of Reality TV

At the beginning of filming, Spirits seemed to come through quite a lot with messages for the crew. Although we'd all laugh, it created difficulties for the editing team, and sometimes made for complicated readings for my clients. So when season two got approved, I begged for my same crew back because it made things so much easier, and that's just what happened.

Filming is just a part of our lives now. We are so used to the cameras and what's happening around us with lights and things, at times we even forget they are with us. In fact, I became so comfortable that they told me they had to bleep out my curse words a lot more often in season two than in season one. Sorry, what you see is what you get with me and with my whole clan!

I don't think filming the TV show has changed who we are at all. I mean, we get recognized when we go to town, and people wave and say hello, but we just are who we are: a close family that goes through the same ups and downs that everyone else does—except we do have close connections to a lot of dead people.

༄ ⊚ ⊚ ༄

AFTERWORD

Wishing You Love, Peace, Forgiveness, and Balance

It's quite possible that, through all these connections that Spirit has guided me to find, my own story will be able to inspire others. As you've seen, my life went from violence and chaos to triumph and celebration . . . and I'm not done yet! I am still a work in progress, as we all are, but I feel 100 times better than I did.

Now it's my sincere wish that this book will resonate with the current generation of seekers, people like you who might also struggle with feelings of panic and anxiety, or the thought that you might be crazy. You might struggle with low self-esteem or addictions or other life challenges that you are ready to heal from.

I encourage you to consider that in your anxiety and internal chaos, in your life of suffering whatever it might be, you are not alone. Your experiences were given to you for a reason. Your soul chose them, and you are here for a bigger purpose than you might be living right now. All of us have spiritual gifts inside us that can cause us grief until we start to listen to them and learn to use them for our greater good.

Don't feel that you have to be afraid or live in shame any longer. You might have made monumentally poor choices in your life, as I certainly did. Yet I was able to heal and rebuild my life out of such shambles, and you can do it, too. I stopped the cycle of tapping and chaos for myself, and I foresee a better life for my children and grandchildren than I could have ever hoped for.

Just remember the most important relationship you are ever going to have is the one *with yourself.* When you begin to heal your inner self, you'll find yourself on a most amazing journey.

I fully expect that your path can take you through your own main keys to a successful and happy life, the same keys that I worked through. As you conquer the universal concepts of *love, peace, forgiveness,* and *balance* in your own way, using your own intuition and your own inner strengths, you will uncover your authentic self. Once you do, everything around you will change.

Trust me. I'm a psychic. *True Story.*

ACKNOWLEDGMENTS

I want to thank my husband, Dave, who has never left my side. We have been through so much, and I am so blessed that we always find the same path in the end. You support every venture I embark on, even the wild and crazy ones. Without your constant support and guidance, all of this would not be possible. I love you to the moon.

To my children, Melissa, Wayne, Jessica, Emily, Keghan, and Mike: Thank you for your unconditional love, everlasting support, and constant entertainment. I love you and all your "triggers." Thank you for picking me to be the mom. XO

To my mom: I am grateful every day that I picked you to be my mom. I thank you for believing in me and always being a constant support through thick and thin. Even when you didn't think I was listening, *I was.* I love you. I am still listening, even though you are now in Spirit. I miss you more than you can know and send love as you continue your journey on the Other Side.

To my brother Kevin, my sister Tracy, and my island family: Thank you for supporting me through it all and putting up with the "craziness" just long enough to have it all make sense. *Who knew?!*

To my best friend, Suzanne: Thank you for being you and for showing me what true friendship means and is. You have taught me what it means to truly laugh and then laugh some more. XO

To my devoted team (Riley, Vanessa, and Tamara): You are all truly Angels in disguise. It takes a special person to balance the life of a medium. Thank you all for being a constant support and helping to navigate through the good, the bad, and the ugly.

To my dearest friend Katherine Hole: You always know just what to say and when to say it. And let's not forget, you're always offering the most amazing place to escape from it all: Pembina Ranch. Thank you for being a true friend and a constant support.

To R and his family: You all taught me love and were the first to show me what a loving home and family can feel like. I am blessed to have known you all, and I am grateful for each moment we shared.

To Don Archibold: Thank you for planting the seed and believing in me.

To my Lark Production family and CORUS Entertainment: Thank you for believing in us and helping us share our lives with the world! We appreciate all you do and the support you have given.

To Tiffany Grabski: When I began writing this book, I knew I'd need a special person to tell all my truths to. Someone who wouldn't judge me, someone I could trust, and someone I would never feel ashamed to expose the good, the bad, and the ugly. Thank you, Tiffany, for listening without judgment or prejudice, and offering me acceptance and love. I am blessed to have you in my life.

To Sonia Choquette: Thank you for believing in me and for teaching me to trust. You are the greatest teacher we can ever have, and I am eternally grateful to you.

To Ryan Kaiser: Thank you for words of encouragement and support, and for being the best business advisor and agent ever! But we still have better hockey players.

To Louise Hay: I am forever grateful and blessed to be a part of Hay House Publishing. The gifts of knowledge that your books and publishing company have given to the world are invaluable. Allowing me to be part of that team is a dream I still cannot truly fathom. Thank you for finding me on the journey.

To Nicolette Salamanca Young at Hay House: You are a saint! Your patience, understanding, and guidance are what every author needs on their writing journey, and I loved working with you. Thank you for *being you.*

To Simone Graham: Thank God for your ability to see my full vision and help continue to mold this story. I am forever grateful and blessed to have you as part of my team, for you truly are a gift to literature.

ABOUT THE AUTHORS

Carmel Joy Baird is a spiritual visionary and a gifted medium, with the ability to convey messages from departed Spirits who are on the Other Side. Through compassion, humor, and love, she provides healing readings to clients who travel to see her from around the world, seeking peace and closure, often after the loss of someone dear to them.

Carmel herself suffered with acute panic and anxiety most of her life until she found peace by discovering her ability to be a medium. In addition to seeing personal clients, she also uses her intuitive abilities within open mediumship events and to assist or advise law enforcement professionals about missing-persons cases. One of her passions is to teach others how to develop their own intuitive gifts, because she believes *we are all psychic.*

Carmel and her husband, Dave, recently completed season two of the reality TV show *Mom's a Medium* (CMT), which hit airwaves in the spring of 2015. The show is set on their acreage in western Canada, where they live with two of their six children and a number of animals, including their beloved horses and dogs.

Website: www.carmeljoybaird.com

Tiffany Grabski is a native Canadian and travel enthusiast whose natural curiosity for life led her into a career as a journalist and writer. Inspired by the people she met along this journey, Tiffany went on to earn her MBA, specializing in sustainable development, at the University of Geneva in Switzerland. She now works at the United Nations and continues to write as a hobby.

.

Printed in the United States
by Baker & Taylor Publisher Services